Praise for *Enjoy Today Own Tom*

"Now you know why Laine is such a dear friend to me: becau___ ___ ___ sands of women find out how to live free, whole, and energized. This *Enjoy Today Own Tomorrow Journal* is one of the greatest tools to help women overcome struggles and discover the power to live their best life now. Laine guides the reader to personalize their healing through the pages of this journal and helps the reader take the exact steps for success."

—Nancy Alcorn, founder and president, Mercy Multiplied

"Laine has such a beautiful heart for helping and lifting up women. I believe this journal is sure to guide us to tap into the amazing life God has planned for us; after all, his plan is way bigger and better than we can ever imagine for ourselves."

—Ali Landry, actress, host, former Miss USA, cofounder
ReShape health and wellness platform

"What a brilliant idea to compile a journal to go along with such a wonderful, heartfelt book, *Enjoy Today Own Tomorrow*! What I appreciate the most, as an avid journaler, are the questions and the divisions: "Reconnect with God," "Realign Your Heart," and "Reactivate Your Faith." Such an insightful combination!"

—Eva Marie Everson, best-selling author and speaker; president,
Word Weavers International

"She's done it again! Laine Lawson Craft: devout lover of people and powerhouse for providing tools to help make the lives of women better. That's why I'm honored to endorse Laine's new journal: because it was written with your personal growth in mind and will surely take you deeper in intimacy with God as you read and jot down how you choose to *Enjoy Today, Own Tomorrow*."

—LaTan Roland Murphy, award-winning author, *Courageous Women of the Bible:
Leaving Behind Fear & Insecurity for a Life of Confidence and Freedom*

"Laine Lawson Craft has done it again! On the heels of her best-selling *Enjoy Today Own Tomorrow* book, this journal offers women—who are ready to find freedom and live whole and healed—the process to start living their best life now! I first heard Laine speak in 2008, and she told everyone in the room, "I love you," Since then I've heard her say it to people she encounters wherever she goes, from service workers to executives, strangers and friends. And I've heard her say it to me. Laine loves deeply from the well of God's unfathomable love, and her passion to minister to women is as real as it gets. I love you, Laine Lawson Craft!"

—Jenny L. Cote, speaker and author, *The Amazing Tales of Max and Liz,*
Epic Order of the Seven

"Laine Lawson Craft has always had a heart for the brokenhearted. Through this *Enjoy Today Own Tomorrow Journal,* women will find the way to heal from the trials of life. The journal takes you down a path where you will discover God intimately and then allow Him to move through the hurts and give you healing. This journal will set you free so that you can live free and love again!"

—Barbara J. Yoder, lead apostle, Shekinah, Regional Apostolic Center

"Laine Lawson Craft is not only a bestselling author but she is also a tried-and-true friend who has walked out what she has written in the pages of this beautiful journal. I love how interactive both her journal and she is with her readers. I believe you will literally begin to enjoy your today and own your tomorrow as you journey with Laine through this healing process, leaving hurts from yesterday in the dust where they belong!"

—Adrienne Cooley, author, *Happy ANYWAY* and *Love ANYWAY*; founder, Happy Sisterhood; host, annual Happy Girl Conference

ENJOY

today

OWN

tomorrow

Journal

ENJOY
today
OWN
tomorrow

Journal

DISCOVER THE POWER TO
LIVE THE LIFE YOU LOVE

LAINE LAWSON CRAFT

ASCENDER
BOOKS
An Imprint of Iron Stream Media

Birmingham, Alabama

Ascender Books
100 Missionary Ridge
Birmingham, AL 35242
An imprint of Iron Stream Media
IronStreamMedia.com

Artist and Cover designed by Kaylee Craft Colbert

ISBN-13: 978-1-56309-497-2
Ebook ISBN: 978-1-56309-507-8

1 2 3 4 5—25 24 23 22 21
Manufactured in the United States of America

DEDICATION

To
Kaylee Craft

To my angel, my daughter, my closest and dearest friend,
who has been the inspiration and encouragement
throughout my journey to be bold and to be the risk-taking
woman that God created me to be.

I love you so dearly, and I am so thankful for all that you are,
for all that you do, and for all that God has purposed to
do through you!

CONTENTS

Acknowledgments ....

Letter to the Reader ix

Week 1: Love, Know, and Activate God in Your Life 1

Week 2: Reconnect When You Are Angry at God 27

Week 3: Reconnect with God When You Are Hurt 53

Week 4: Reconnect with God When the People of the Church Hurt You 79

Week 5: Realigning Begins with Your Heart 103

Week 6: What Spiritual Realignment Looks Like 129

Week 7: Realigning Your Life...155

Week 8: Discovering and Reactivating the Power Within You 177

Week 9: Reactivate by Paying It Forward.. 203

Week 10: My Reconnect, Realign, Reactivate Story........................... 229

Group Discussion Guide 255

Stay Connected with Laine 261

Promise Cards 263

LETTER TO THE READER

I am so humbled you've chosen to join me on a ten-week journey of healing. My heart was so touched that thousands of women read my best-selling, *Enjoy Today Own Tomorrow* book. This book guided women down a pathway that gave them the ability to walk out of their hurts into healing successfully. Now, they are enjoying their day and owning their tomorrow.

Also, my heart was warmed when many women asked for a deeper path to guide them down a personal healing journey. So I designed and created a journal to help encourage greater revelations and applications to reconnect lives with God, realign hearts to His, and reactivate faith daily in an interactive and intimate way.

The journal is designed for ten weeks, which represent the ten chapters in the book. You will be challenged daily to pray, answer introspective questions, read scriptures, and reflect over the week's discoveries and applications. In addition to this, you will have specific declaration cards and promise cards that are God's truths for you to speak over and into your lives, opening up the eyes of your heart to hear God speak directly to you. You will begin to see your life in a new way, open yourself up like never before, and live life to the fullest through God's love for you!

I am certain that healing is possible. Hope is available. You will discover a deeper love of God and personalize your own healing journey. I am so thrilled to be with you as you find purpose to your past, hope for your future, and the power to live your best life now.

I pray that you will be touched by the extravagant love of God throughout the pages of this journal and that you will live a life you love—whole, healed, and free!

I love y'all!
From my heart to yours,
Laine

Week 1

LOVE, KNOW, AND ACTIVATE GOD IN YOUR LIFE

From My Heart to Yours

Dearest sister, this week I have a powerful prayer for you. As my friend, I pray that you can observe where you are in life and begin to see that God loves you extravagantly right where you are. I pray that you see how He desperately pursues *you* to commune with Him today.

Let Us Pray

Dear Lord, I pray today to ask that you please reveal yourself in a greater way this week so that we can hear, feel, and experience an intimate touch by you alone.

Lord, we know that we can't hide from you and that you already know everything. We know you are the God who sees us and knows us intimately. Please help us find the courage to run back into your outstretched arms and allow you to move through our broken hearts so that we can find healing.

Lord, we thank you for your unlimited mercy and grace poured over our lives. We ask now that you would be so gracious and forgive us of our sins. Cleanse our hearts. Guide us, Lord, through the process of healing as we reconnect with you—in knowing who you are, realigning our hearts to yours, and reactivating the power within us to walk out of our hurts into healing. In Jesus's name, the name above all names, we pray. Amen.

Introduction

My life plummeted when circumstances around me got tough. My marriage was dead, my children faced life-threatening illnesses, and my husband's business was about to go under. As I said in *Enjoy Today, Own Tomorrow*: "Truthfully, I was falling apart on the inside and out. I kept thinking in the same circles. How did I get here? Where did I go wrong? Where is the life I dreamed of? Where was this God I needed, and was this His plan for my life? Who was God anyway?"

At my lowest point, I began to really look at my life, my relationships, and most importantly, my relationship with God. I asked more questions: "Who was this God? Did He really love me? Because if He did love me this was an awful way to show it—leaving me in a pit of powerless despair." I set out not just to find the answers but "to find healing at all costs."

That process led to identifying three things I had to do: reconnect with God, realign my heart and life to abide in God's love, and reactive my life through discovering God's power within me.

This week, take account of where your life is at this moment in time. Use these questions and others provided during the daily devotions to see your life in a new way and from a different perspective. This can be the beginning for you to discover how you can live your life to the fullest through God's love for you!

Day One

My journey began by honestly asking the question, *Do I know God personally and intimately?* I discovered:

I did not have a relationship with the God described in Scripture. The words written in the Bible were inspired by the very breath of God and are alive today, but I did not know His character, His thoughts, His unconditional love for me, or His supernatural power. I only heard what the culture I inhabited had told me about God. My mind was full of generalities, but I did not have a clue how He related to me in a personal way. I began to realize that the best life today can only be achieved by connecting intimately with God, aligning myself within His love, and activating the power found within Him. (*Enjoy Today Own Tomorrow*)

Reconnect with God: Do you just know God or do you have a personal relationship with Him? Below are synonyms for the word *intimate*. Circle those that describe your closest relationship with someone:

cherished	dear	familiar
close	deep	innermost
confidant	devoted	nearest
constant	faithful	personal

Review your responses above. Do they describe not only your closest human relationship but your relationship with God as well? Does your evaluation leave you wanting to reconnect in your relationship with God? Why?

· ·

· ·

· ·

· ·

· ·

· ·

Realign your heart: Read Psalm 8 below from the New King James Version and underline each word or phrase that describes the relationship that God desires to have with us. Remember that God *created* you to be in relationship with Him.

O Lord, our Lord,
How excellent is Your name in all the earth,
Who have set Your glory above the heavens!

Out of the mouth of babes and nursing infants
You have ordained strength,
Because of Your enemies,
That You may silence the enemy and the avenger.

When I consider Your heavens, the work of Your fingers,
The moon and the stars, which You have ordained,
What is man that You are mindful of him,
And the son of man that You visit him?
For You have made him a little lower than the angels,
And You have crowned him with glory and honor.

YOU HAVE MADE HIM TO HAVE DOMINION OVER THE WORKS OF YOUR HANDS;
You have put all things under his feet,
All sheep and oxen—
Even the beasts of the field,
The birds of the air,
And the fish of the sea
That pass through the paths of the seas.

O LORD, OUR LORD,
How excellent is Your name in all the earth!

Describe the relationship you would like to have with God.

Reactivate your faith: God desires that relationship with you as well. If fact, He desires so much more. Begin now to pray intentionally for God to reveal Himself and His desires to you through this study.

"I began to realize that the best life today can only be achieved by connecting intimately with God."

Day Two

*O*nce I recognized what I wanted in my relationship with God, I set out in brokenness and hopelessness to find it. I dared God to show up to me. I dared myself:

> I challenged my messed-up heart and broken life to believe in the God who created the universe. I had to risk that He would come through and help me to live the life He promised for all through His Son. I visualized the water of the Red Sea, which God parted for Moses, when more than one million people passed through to a new life. I told myself, "I'll tap my toe, and if the water parts, then God will lead me to the next step." (*Enjoy Today Own Tomorrow*)

Reconnect with God: What does it mean to "dare God"? Synonyms for *dare* include *defy*, *provoke*, *stump*, and *taunt*. Why do you think I was willing to dare God? How does daring God show a level of faith? How can daring God lead to reconnecting with Him?

. . . .

. . . .

. . . .

. . . .

. . . .

. . . .

Realign your heart: The word *realign* means to take something to a new place or to take something back to a former place. That means that to realign your relationship with God could mean returning to a time when that relationship was healthy and growing. Or it could mean that you need to do something new to realign yourself with God. Which of these possibilities best describes where you are today with your relationship with God? What would it take for you to realign yourself with Him?

Reactivate with God: I explained that when I made my first timid step toward God, I realized God wants that step from all of us. How could reactivating your faith with God change your life?

Read Psalm 139. God knows you intimately. He knows your secrets, your desires, your strengths, and your weaknesses. He knows what's good in your life, and He knows what's not so good. Knowing all that, is there anything keeping you from taking that first step toward Him? What are you willing to do today to move toward reconnecting with God?

....

....

....

....

....

....

Ask God to give you the wisdom to know what that first step is and the courage to take it.

"I had to risk that He would come through and help me to live the life He promised for all through His Son."

Day Three

I poignantly described how God showed up for me while I was on my knees in prayer:

I simply cried out my pain from the deepest recesses of my heart. Then suddenly there was an overwhelming peace and warmth that flowed throughout my whole body. My tears immediately abated. I knew God had touched me, and my heart accepted the warmth of His love for the very first time in my adult life. (*Enjoy Today Own Tomorrow*)

Reconnect with God: Many adults have gone through what I have experienced. They think they have faith because they know about God, but they don't have a personal relationship with Him when they need Him most. Does that describe your journey? Why?

. . . .

. . . .

. . . .

. . . .

. . . .

. . . .

Have you ever felt that God wasn't there for you when you needed Him? If you have, what have you done to reconnect with Him?

Realign your heart: I wrote that I faced this part of my journey by surrendering my heart to God. Recall your journey with the Lord:

When did you accept Jesus as your Lord and Savior? Were you a child or an adult? How did your age and maturity affect your salvation experience?

How did that decision impact your life immediately?

How has that decision impacted your life lately?

. . . .

. . . .

. . . .

. . . .

. . . .

. . . .

Based on your journey to date, does your heart need to be realigned with His? Why?

. . . .

. . . .

. . . .

. . . .

. . . .

. . . .

Reactivate your faith: Read Psalm 51. David pleaded for God's mercy in the face of his own transgressions and begged for God to cleanse and restore him back to God. Can you relate to David's request? Record your own feelings of guilt or rejoicing in God's saving grace in your life. Pray through verses 10–12, asking God to reactivate your faith and help you reclaim the joy of your salvation.

"I knew God had touched me, and my heart accepted the warmth of His love for the very first time in my adult life."

Day Four

I realized that I battled the lies of the enemy, even as I battled my way back to God. I wrote:

> Is the enemy lying to you? Are you allowing him to persuade you of the impossibility that God could ever love you? The devil almost had me convinced that I could never be loved unconditionally by God. This is a lie from the greatest liar. Don't fall for it another second. His tactics are a ploy to keep you from God's love and His power meant to transform your life. (*Enjoy Today Own Tomorrow*)

Reconnect with God: Satan uses three things to pull me away from God: he keeps me busy with fear, anxiety, and hopelessness; he uses my cultural complacency to dull my senses about what God expects of me; and he uses personal relationships to distract me.

How have you seen yourself pulled away from God—either through relationships, busyness, or complacency? What direct impact has that had on your relationship with God?

Realign your heart: I used the disciplines of prayer and scripture study to combat the lies of the enemy and to realign my heart with God's. Based on my suggestions from this chapter, what study ideas have been presented that could help you strengthen your own time of study and prayer?

Reactivate your faith: It is important to spend time with God every day in order to reactivate your faith. How would your faith be strengthened if you made time daily to spend with God in prayer and scripture study?

What would it take for you to make daily study and prayer a priority?

. . . .

. . . .

. . . .

. . . .

. . . .

. . . .

The author of Psalm 91 outlines what it is like to dwell in the shadow of the almighty God. Read Psalm 91 and list the words and phrases that call attention to God's constant protection and to finding refuge near Him. Then, read it aloud as a prayer, asking God to teach you to study His scripture in ways that allow you to dwell within His refuge.

. . . .

. . . .

. . . .

. . . .

. . . .

"God is a God of overflowing abundance."

Day Five

$\mathcal{I}$ ended the first chapter of *Enjoy Today Own Tomorrow* by outlining three truths about God. These truths can guide us in the process of reconnecting with God, realigning our hearts, and reactivating our faith.

Reconnect with God: The first truth about God that I shared is that "He has no limits. He is infinite. There is no way to measure Him. God is a God of overflowing abundance. This attribute and truth mean we can experience His supernatural overflow personally. He is always ready and eager to give generously and fill whatever need we may have."

Since God is infinite, how can you relate to Him? For suggestions, read Psalm 103:8–12.

. . . .

. . . .

. . . .

. . . .

. . . .

. . . .

Realign your heart: The second truth I shared is that "God is our Father, our guide, and our companion for life. God longs for each of us to know our identity in Him, specifically that we are His child. . . . God's love exceeds that of any dad on earth. In fact, it is so extravagant and unique that it's almost incomprehensible."

What is your identity in God? How has He sovereignly called you into His family?

. . . .

. . . .

. . . .

. . . .

. . . .

. . . .

How does God serve as your guide and companion? Is He a silent partner, an involved guide, or a constant companion? Why?

. . . .

. . . .

. . . .

. . . .

. . . .

Reactivate your faith: The third truth about God that I shared is, "God is in sovereign control. Surrendering our will to His, and having faith, is the ultimate way to a successful life. Faith pleases God. There are blessings and rewards for all who diligently seek Him, know Him, and exercise faith through living like Him. When we live out these truths, then no one or nothing can stop us."

Read that quotation again. Have you been the recipient of God's blessings and rewards? Have you diligently sought Him, worked to know Him, and lived your life in ways that reflect Him?

....

....

....

....

....

....

Read Psalm 103:1–5. Read these verses in two or three other translations and write out the one verse that speaks most clearly to you right now. Using that verse as a guide, pray for God to show you His abundant blessings as you seek Him.

....

....

....

....

....

....

"I battled the lies of the enemy, even as I battled my way back to God."

Weekend Reflection

You've spent this week evaluating your relationship with God. That can be a difficult, even exhausting, process. But if you asked yourself the tough questions in this chapter and if you answered those questions honestly, you are ready to move forward in developing and strengthening your relationship with God.

Over the weekend, journal about this week's experiences with these prompts:

What have you learned about your relationship with God right now?

. . . .

. . . .

. . . .

. . . .

. . . .

What feelings have you experienced during this process?

· ·

· ·

· ·

· ·

· ·

What do you want your relationship with God to be like?

· ·

· ·

· ·

· ·

· ·

What steps are you prepared to take to grow in your relationship with God?

· ·

· ·

· ·

· ·

WEEKEND Meditation from *Enjoy Today, Own Tomorrow* Declaration Cards

THE LORD IS CLOSE TO THE BROKENHEARTED
and saves those who are crushed in spirit.

Psalm 34:18

Take your time with journaling, meditation, and prayer before you move into week 2. Allow God to speak to you about your relationship with Him and His desires for you.

RECONNECT WHEN YOU ARE ANGRY AT GOD

From My Heart to Yours

Dearest sister, my prayer this week for you is that you know God is bigger than our anger at Him. God is not upset at us when we get angry with Him.

Let Us Pray

Dear God, thank you for loving us despite all our anger. Thank you for never giving up on us. Lord, help us turn back to you. We know that when we confess our anger, we are bringing it into the light. Anger can no longer separate us, Lord. We confess our anger and hand over our wounds this week so that you can begin to mend our hearts.

Lord, please be with us as we walk out a hard week. Teach us how to pray and communicate with you so that we can find deliverance from our anger. Help us write down our emotions in this journal as we learn to let go of these negative feelings and hand them over to you. Lord, help our faith to be strengthened so that we can believe that we can have a whole and healed heart.

In the powerful name of Jesus, amen.

Introduction

Anger toward God is not new. Centuries of followers have struggled with dealing with tragedy and suffering and questioned why God wasn't doing something to make it better. But despite how many people have experienced such anger at God, few are willing to admit that anger to others. Why is that?

It's easy to understand our frustration. How do we understand an illness that takes the life of a small child or an accident that takes the lives of an entire family? How do we understand the incomprehensible?

I documented my own journey with anger toward God:

We are often left with more questions than answers. . . .

. . . Why does a God who loves us allow such terrible things to happen? . . . The best answer any human can supply is that we will never comprehend God in His infinite wisdom. We will never know the end of humanity's story, but He does. We are temporal-minded. God is omniscient. . . .

. . . The bottom line is God does not make bad things happen. God doesn't hurt people. God never wishes harm. How could anyone love God if he or she believed those things about Him? (*Enjoy Today Own Tomorrow*)

This week, allow God to show you places in your life where you've allowed tragedy and suffering to hurt your relationship with Him. Open yourself to the Holy God who loves you more than you will ever comprehend. Be willing to let go of anger and hurt from circumstances and experiences that have pushed you away from Him.

Day One

I explained that "moving through the process of forgiving God, turning back, and reconnecting to Him is not a one-step method. But it does take only one second to decide that we can quit harboring anger—period. The same life-altering second of emotional trauma that flooded our hearts with anger toward God can be defeated with a one-second decision to release our anger at Him" (*Enjoy Today Own Tomorrow*). The question for you, right this second: Are you ready to let go of your anger toward God *NOW*?

Reconnect with God: I outlined three steps for reconnecting with God despite your anger, realigning your heart with His, and reactivating your faith in Him. The first step is to decide that it's time to let go of your resentment against God. Therapists have found common signs of long-held anger and resentment. Review the list of common signs below and check any of those that you have experienced in your relationship with God:

  ➢ Strong emotional feelings when you think about what happened
  ➢ Continual thoughts about what happened that caused your anger
  ➢ Regret for what has happened
  ➢ Fear of dealing with your emotions
  ➢ Stress in your relationship
  ➢ Feelings that you no longer count or are inadequate
      (List paraphrased from "Resentment," GoodTherapy,
      https://www.goodtherapy.org/blog/psychpedia/resentment.)

Are any of these signs evident in your life and your relationship with God? In order to reconnect with God, you have to turn to Him. Only God can heal your pain and help you let go of your anger toward Him.

Realign your heart: The second step is to simply confess your anger toward God to someone. The phrase *simply confess* may be a bit of an oxymoron. True confession is not simple—it can be painful to open up the wounds that caused your anger. But just like lancing an infected abscess, only by opening that wound can God bring healing to your heart.

Think of people who can understand what you've experienced and who can understand the pain you are in. Write their names below:

. . . .

. . . .

. . . .

. . . .

. . . .

Now, ask God to show you the person that you should contact. Remember that just because you've been angry with God does not mean that He is angry with you. Trust Him to guide you to the person who can help support you through this journey of realigning your heart with His. And follow through. Contact the person God has identified. Set up time to talk over coffee. Or meet somewhere more private if you know you'll be emotional. Start the process so you can be assured of support over the next days and weeks.

Reactivate your faith: The third step is to "choose to surrender our pain and share our anger with God." I found out that "when we offer our anger to Him, He is able to remake us. God begins to lovingly and patiently put the shattered pieces of our hearts and lives back together" (*Enjoy Today Own Tomorrow*).

Read Psalm 13:1–6 and see yourself in David's words. David's confession shows the depth of his hurt, his pain, and his despair. Use David's words to help you form your confession to God. If you are able, write out your confession to God. Use it to lance the spiritual abscesses in your life and give them the opportunity to heal. If you are not ready to put your pain in writing, speak it aloud before God. Confess your anger that He didn't remove the circumstances you've been through. Admit your feelings. Ask God to guide you through this process so you can reconnect to Him, realign your heart with His, and reactivate your faith in Him.

"Trust Him to guide you to the person who can help support you through this journey of realigning your heart with His."

Day Two

I made the case that "prayer changes outcomes":

Research shows those who regularly focus on God's love are less stressed and even experience reduced blood pressure. Prayer actually affects the part of the brain associated with focus. There is also increased activity in the part of our brain associated with love, compassion, and empathy. (*Enjoy Today Own Tomorrow*)

I outlined three patterns of prayer to help reconnect us to God. For the next three days, you'll have the opportunity to use each pattern as you work to strengthen and renew your relationship with God through prayer.

Reconnect with God: The first pattern is a thirty-minute time of prayer that is structured in short designated increments. Use this outline as you pray:

5 minutes: Prayerfully listen to and come into the presence of God through praise and worship music or reading scripture.

5 minutes: Repent before God and request His mercy and forgiveness. Ask God what He wants you to do for Him.

5 minutes: Pray for the kingdom of God, the church, and family members who are unsaved. Pray that God's will be done on earth.

5 minutes: Pray for the local church, for local pastors and their families, and for church members. Pray for unity in working together to reach the lost and the hurting.

3 minutes: Pray for your lost family members and friends who need salvation, for broken and sick family members and friends who need healing, and for you to be able to forgive those who have hurt you.

7 minutes: Spend these last minutes being still and listening for God.

As you conclude your time of prayer, journal about the experience with these questions:

How did you feel yourself reconnecting to God during this time of prayer?

. . . .

. . . .

. . . .

. . . .

. . . .

. . . .

What did that feel like emotionally?

. . . .

. . . .

. . . .

. . . .

. . . .

Realign your heart: As you continue to journal, consider these questions about realigning your heart to His:

What was revealed to you about God's heart?

How did your heart realign with God's heart during prayer?

Can your heart remain aligned with God's without the discipline of prayer? Why?

· ·

· ·

· ·

· ·

· ·

· ·

Reactivate your faith: Meditate on these words from Psalm 61:1–3:

HEAR MY CRY, O GOD;
  listen to my prayer.

FROM THE ENDS OF THE EARTH I CALL TO YOU,
  I call as my heart grows faint;
  lead me to the rock that is higher than I.
For you have been my refuge,
  a strong tower against the foe.

God desires your relationship with Him. God longs for your heart to be aligned with His. And God wants to use your faith to bring glory to Him. Reflect on how this prayer experience has brought all three of those statements into focus for you.

"God desires your relationship with Him. God longs for your heart to be aligned with His."

Day Three

The second prayer pattern is similar to the first but is much less structured. In the second prayer, I give suggestions of what to pray for and about, but the prayer itself is free from structure and limitation. The underlying theme of the prayer is thanksgiving.

Reconnect with God: It can be helpful to write down your prayer needs before you begin to pray. Then, as you pray, use these prompts as God directs you:

1. Pray with thanksgiving for all that God has done and will do.
2. Pray with gratitude for the good things of God in your life.
3. Pray with praise and adoration for who God is in your life.
4. Pray through worship music that speaks about God's character.
5. Pray for God's forgiveness for anything you need to be forgiven for.
6. Pray for God to show you His will for your life.
7. Pray by being silent, listening for God's direction.

As you conclude your time of prayer, journal about the experience with these questions:

How did you feel yourself reconnecting to God during this time of prayer?

What did that feel like emotionally?

· ·

· ·

· ·

· ·

· ·

· ·

Realign your heart: As you continue to journal, consider these questions about realigning your heart to His:

What was revealed to you about God's heart during this time of prayer?

· ·

· ·

· ·

· ·

· ·

How did your heart realign with God's heart during prayer?

Reactivate your faith: Meditate on David's words from Psalm 63:1:

You, God, are my God,
   earnestly I seek you;
I thirst for you,
   my whole being longs for you,
in a dry and parched land
   where there is no water.

God desires for you to desire Him. He doesn't want to be an afterthought or an inconvenience. He wants you to be connected the way you were created to connect to Him, to be a person after "God's own heart" as David was, and to live in a way that expresses your deep and abiding love for and faith in Him. Reflect on how this prayer experience has brought all three of those statements into focus for you.

"He wants you to be connected the way you were created to connect to Him, to be a person after 'God's own heart.'"

Day Four

The third pattern is a thirty-minute time of prayer that is structured in shorter designated increments than the first pattern and is based on scripture.

Reconnect with God: Use this outline as you pray:

5 minutes: Read a psalm and dialog with God about what you've read. Or pray the psalm to God.

1 minute: Read in Proverbs and dialog with God about what you've read. Or pray the proverb to God.

2 minutes: Pray in praise and thanksgiving, listing the things you are thankful for.

1 minute: Pray in confession, noting the times you've felt distant from God over the past 24 hours.

5 minutes: Pray in intercession for our nation and our world, for national revival, for our military, for wisdom for our leaders, and for those who do not know Jesus.

2 minutes: Memorize scripture.

5 minutes: Be still in prayer. Slow your breathing to increase your awareness of God's presence.

2 minutes: Read a section of the New Testament.

7 minutes: Pray in connection with nature, going outside or to a window. Meditate on God's created world in your view.

As you conclude your time of prayer, journal about the experience with these questions:

How did you feel yourself reconnecting to God during this time of prayer?

....

....

....

....

....

....

What did that feel like emotionally?

....

....

....

....

....

Realign your heart: As you continue to journal, consider these questions about realigning your heart to His:

What was revealed to you about God's heart through this time of prayer?

. . . .

. . . .

. . . .

. . . .

. . . .

. . . .

How did your heart realign with God's heart during prayer?

. . . .

. . . .

. . . .

. . . .

. . . .

Reactivate your faith: Meditate on David's words from Psalm 23:1–4. You probably memorized this psalm as a child, but this time, allow God to speak to your heart in a new way through it:

THE LORD IS MY SHEPHERD, I LACK NOTHING.
  He makes me lie down in green pastures,
he leads me beside quiet waters,
  he refreshes my soul.
He guides me along the right paths
  for his name's sake.
Even though I walk
  through the darkest valley,
I will fear no evil,
  for you are with me;
your rod and your staff,
  they comfort me.

The Twenty-Third Psalm has been used in countless funerals to give comfort and hope. It is also a powerful picture of an active faith—a faith that depends upon God's guidance, God's presence and protection, and God's comfort. Reflect on how this prayer experience has brought all three of those statements into focus for you.

"Allow God to speak to your heart in a new way."

Day Five

You've had three different prayer opportunities over the past three days. Probably, all three stretched you a little, and maybe even pushed you out of your prayer comfort zone. In *Enjoy Today Own Tomorrow*, I pointed out that "any pattern you develop on your own is just as good—or better! The critical point is to find a way to remain consistent in your personal prayer life" (23).

As you consider how to develop consistency in your own prayer life, consider three specific prayer requests that I suggest we use when we are angry at God.

Reconnect with God: The first specific prayer request is to pray for God's comfort while we are struggling. I explained, "He comforts us in all trials (2 Corinthians 1:4). He is there when it seems as though no one else cares or is able to relate. God always comforts the brokenhearted (Psalm 34:18)" (*Enjoy Today Own Tomorrow*).

Just as it can be hard to connect meaningfully to someone when we are mad at him or her, it can be difficult to find the words to communicate with God when we are angry or hurt. I suggest simply asking God to put His arms around you since you have no words of your own.

Have you tried that? How has God reconnected with you when you didn't have the words to reconnect with Him?

. . . .

. . . .

. . . .

. . . .

Realign your heart: The second specific prayer request I suggest we use is to pray against our fear. "When facing anything overwhelming, fear begins to grip us. Sometimes it can . . . make us assume we are powerless. This is why we must reconnect to the power source of the entire universe. . . . God actually helps us rise above our fears and relieves our anger and pain as we pray" (*Enjoy Today Own Tomorrow*).

Fear can compromise faith. I suggest going back to God's Word to strengthen our faith when it is being compromised by fear. Use a Bible concordance to search for verses about faith and fear and list what you find below. To get you started, look at Hebrews 11:1, Ephesians 2:8-9, and Psalm 56:3. Continue until you have a healthy list of verses to draw upon.

Choose one of the Scripture verses you've listed above and commit it to memory. Write it on an index card that can stay in your purse or briefcase. Reflect on it each morning and evening. Use it as a constant reminder of what it means to realign your heart with God's.

Reactivate your faith: Faith is the assurance that God's promises will come to be.

If God said it, then we must believe He will perform it. If God promises to do something, He will do it because it is impossible for Him to lie. Human beings break their promises, but God does not. . . . It's hard to have faith that God will come through for us when our world has fallen apart around us. In those moments, we must remember that God has also promised to get us through all trials." (*Enjoy Today Own Tomorrow*)

When has your faith been compromised by fear? Make a quick list of times when your faith seemed to fail you because the circumstances in your life were so scary.

· ·

· ·

· ·

· ·

· ·

· ·

How did the assurance of God's promises help you through that time? What did you learn about your faith through that process?

· ·

· ·

· ·

· ·

· ·

Your faith is a gift of God, and it is not to be taken lightly. Consider these encouragements from the English Standard Version:

Second Timothy 1:7: "For God gave us a spirit not of fear but of power and love and self-control."

First John 4:18a: "There is no fear in love, but perfect love casts out fear."

Psalm 34:4: "I sought the LORD and he answered me / and delivered me from all my fears."

Your faith is a sign of your relationship with God. Ask God to help you grow in faith, not fear, through the circumstances and trials in your life.

"Find a way to remain consistent in your personal prayer life."

Weekend Reflection

This week, you've explored some deep issues—anger, resentment, prayer, fear, and faith. You may be emotionally exhausted from dredging up things you'd rather not face. You've possibly done some difficult, emotionally taxing work. Congratulations! God will honor your work, your honesty, your vulnerability, and your progress.

Over the weekend, I encourage you to rest in the Lord. Listen to praise and worship music. Spend time outdoors, and allow God's creation to rejuvenate your soul. And, then, when you are relaxed and rested, journal about this week's experiences with these prompts:

What have you learned about your relationship with God right now?

. . . .

. . . .

. . . .

. . . .

. . . .

. . . .

What feelings have you experienced during this process?

....

....

....

....

....

What do you want your relationship with God to be like?

....

....

....

....

....

What steps are you prepared to take to grow in your relationship with God?

....

....

....

....

....

WEEKEND Meditation from *Enjoy Today, Own Tomorrow* Promise Cards

DO NOT BE AFRAID OR DISCOURAGED, FOR THE LORD WILL PERSONALLY GO AHEAD OF YOU. HE WILL BE WITH YOU; HE WILL NEITHER FAIL YOU NOR ABANDON YOU.

Deuteronomy 31:8 (NLT)

Take your time with journaling, meditation, and prayer before you move into week 3. Allow God to speak to you about your relationship with Him and His desires for you.

Week 3

RECONNECT WITH GOD WHEN YOU ARE HURT

From My Heart to Yours

Dearest sister, one of the toughest parts of life is that we all get hurt. No one gets through this life without pain. It is terribly difficult when we get wounded by those closest to us or other believers. The key to overcoming these wounds is to face them, not to bury them, and then to process them so that we can be healed.

Let Us Pray

Dear God, we know that you would never leave us in our brokenness. Father, we thank you that you literally capture our tears and feel every pain we experience. We thank you for your examples in the Bible that help guide us on how to heal when others hurt us.

Lord, thank you that your words enable us to find encouragement and have a new level of hope that we will overcome. Thank you, Lord, that we can remind ourselves of hurts you have healed us from in the past and then know you will do it again. You are trustworthy! Help us forgive our offenders just as you forgive us of our sins. We know your healing power is waiting for us, and we call upon it today.

We love you, Lord. In Jesus's name, amen.

Introduction

All of us have been hurt by others. We've suffered pain from their actions or their words. We have experienced the pain of shattered relationships. Sadly, those who have the power to hurt us the most are often those we know best—family, significant others, coworkers, or good friends. The pain of loss can seem unbearable.

In my book, I discussed how medical research has documented that emotional and social pain is usually harder to get through than physical pain. Dr. Kip Williams from Purdue University explains: "Social pain has the unique ability to come back over and over again, whereas physical pain lingers only as an awareness that it was indeed at one time painful."

I described why this difference in pain is so important to understand: "Many of us try to 'stuff' pain deep within so that we don't have to feel it. Inevitably, we find it will resurface in a different manifestation. Consequently, we end up hurting all over again or even hurting others." Many of us try to just forget what happened and move on with our lives, hoping the pain will just go away. Unfortunately, that usually doesn't happen. "How are we to correctly deal with emotional pain? How do we recover when the people closest to us wound our hearts?" (*Enjoy Today Own Tomorrow*)

This week, we'll look at those questions and more. As we begin, ask God to reveal the hurts and wounds in your life that you've tried so hard to forget. And then, get ready for God to lead you in the process of healing—in a way that will change your life forever.

Day One

It's impossible not to get hurt and wounded in our evil world. You've already been wounded in your life and might be still trying to move past it. In *Enjoy Today, Own Tomorrow*, I stressed that "one of the best ways to heal from these traumatic wounds is to dig deep in the word of God and access His healing power." I also underscored that many who are wounded will also need professional counseling and possibly even medication "coupled with the spiritual access of God to provide a combined approach to complete healing."

Reconnect with God: I wrote, "The Creator of the universe has felt our pain within the beating of His own heart." Read that statement again and reflect on it below:

What emotional pain has God felt?

....

....

....

....

....

....

What emotional pain has God felt for your pain?

. . . .

. . . .

. . . .

. . . .

. . . .

. . . .

Were those questions hard to answer? The first question should bring back pictures of how God sent His Son to us knowing that His Son would suffer rejection and hatred, experience humiliation, and die a horrible death. There is nothing you've experienced that is greater than the pain God has endured for you.

The second question should remind you that God *cares for you*. There is nothing that you will ever experience that God doesn't know about and care about.

I wrote, "He hates that we have pain at all. But God uses our pain. He loves us so intimately that He shared His pain to rescue and reconcile us back to Him."

Realign your heart: I wrote, "When we reconnect with God, through meditating on the steps of His own pain and by studying the stories throughout the Bible, we find ways to work through our own pain and reach recovery. The process of emotional healing can only come from following God's wisdom and example."

Think about how Jesus suffered. Consider how deeply God, who is the author of emotion, felt all that happened to Jesus. What does this tell you about how deeply God also cares for you?

. . . .

. . . .

. . . .

. . . .

. . . .

. . . .

Reactivate your faith: Read John 3:16. Then think about it this way: God loved the world so much He sent His only Son—His unique Son, the only Son He has ever had or will ever have—so that whosoever believes in Him will have eternal life. As you close out today's study, pray through John 3:16 using these statements:

1. For God so loves ME that He sent His only begotten Son—His unique Son, His one and only Son, the only Son He would ever have—so that when I believe in Him I will not perish, but I will have eternal life.
2. For God loves ME so much that He sent His only begotten Son—His Son that He felt deeply about—to show me how much He does love me.
3. For God loves ME so much that He cares about the wounds and pain that I am carrying and wants me to heal.

"There is nothing that you will ever experience that God doesn't know about and care about."

Day Two

The Book of Genesis recorded how Joseph, the favored son, was betrayed by his jealous brothers and sold into slavery. It's hard to even imagine how deep Joseph's hurt went. Yet, the story of Joseph's time in Egypt is an example of how to seek reconciliation and offer forgiveness, despite deep emotional pain. How did Joseph find the ability to forgive and to move past his hurt? As I explained, "Joseph always kept his eyes on God. Joseph believed, in his heart, in the providence of God. He knew God always had a plan for him and that it would somehow work out for Joseph's best. . . . Every trial he faced further molded Joseph's character to fulfill God's destiny for him" (*Enjoy Today Own Tomorrow*).

Forgiveness seldom comes easily. And it doesn't happen without hard work and spiritual growth. Only through God can we learn to forgive others the way God has forgiven us.

Reconnect with God: Forgiveness is a choice. We can choose to forgive someone who has hurt us deeply, or we can choose to hold on to the hurt, the pain, and the loss of trust.

How do you make choices? Are you spontaneous and quick to decide? Do you consider all the options and decide only after you have all the information possible?

What does your process of decision-making tell you about yourself?

....

....

....

....

....

Did you mention seeking God's direction in your decision-making process above? Why?

....

....

....

....

....

Realign your heart: Sometimes we forget the pain and humiliation that Jesus faced. Search Jesus's experiences in Matthew 26:47–50, 65–68; 27:27–31, 32–37, 45–46 and record the things He endured below:

....

....

....

....

....

Jesus allowed all this pain and humiliation to be heaped upon Him. He didn't have to accept it or tolerate it because He had the power to avoid it. Yet, He chose to take it so we would receive God's ultimate forgiveness and redemption.

Reactivate your faith: Read John 3:16 again. This time, reflect on the phrase, "For God so loved the world that He sent His only begotten Son." Then, pray:

1. Acknowledge that sending His Son to us, knowing what His Son would have to endure, cost God emotionally.
2. Acknowledge that Jesus coming to us was a choice on His part to take on your sins, your pain, and your hurt, and that it cost Him physically and emotionally.
3. Ask God to teach you how to choose to forgive those who have hurt you.

"Forgiveness seldom comes easily. And it doesn't happen without hard work and spiritual growth."

Day Three

*B*esides struggling with giving forgiveness, we can also face discouragement. I pointed out, "Discouragement can often paralyze us when people closest to us hurt us. The inability to forgive, bitterness, resentment, and discouragement can become stumbling blocks" (*Enjoy Today Own Tomorrow*).

Today, be ready to find answers to my questions:

➢ How do we process discouragement when hurting?
➢ How do we fight to bring ourselves out of the pit of being discouraged?

Reconnect with God: Discouragement can be understood as hopelessness, disappointment, dejection, and sadness. Notice how each of those descriptors is opposite to what you feel when you are connected to God. I explained, "Primary symptoms manifest in continual feelings of being defeated and overwhelmed. The ravaging cost of these emotional tidal waves is that they take away all of our life energy."

Think of a time when you have faced similar feelings (and it may be right now). How did those feelings make it difficult for you to connect with God?

. . . .

. . . .

. . . .

. . . .

. . . .

Is it difficult to come near to God when you are feeling defeated or hopeless? Why?

. . . .

. . . .

. . . .

. . . .

. . . .

. . . .

Realign your heart: The Bible is full of hope for the hopeless. Read through these verses and choose one to memorize and hold on to in times of hopelessness:

Psalm 33:18	Jeremiah 29:11
Psalm 33:22	Mark 9:23
Psalm 71:14	Romans 15:13
Psalm 130:5	Colossians 3:1–2
Isaiah 40:31	Hebrews 10:23

Write your chosen verse on several index cards and put them in places you'll see daily, such as taped to your bathroom mirror, on your car's dashboard, or in your kitchen. Don't just memorize the verse but think about it throughout your day. Claim the promise and use it as an antidote of hope against the hopelessness.

Finally, begin to journal about the feelings of hopelessness and the promise of hope. You'll be able to look back on how claiming God's hope in your life made a difference in your ability to overcome hopelessness and discouragement.

Reactivate your faith: I discovered that speaking words of encouragement to ourselves is also an important step in overcoming discouragement. I wrote, "It can be challenging, sometimes, to say kind or positive things to or about ourselves. But what we mentally tell ourselves has everything to do with how we experience people or events." These words are supported by psychologists who have found that we are able to cushion how negative feelings impact us through changing how we speak to ourselves.

Is your inner dialog positive or negative? Do you hold on to personal guilt for things that you may not even be guilty of? How do you think negative thoughts are holding you back from being able to reconnect with God and reaffirm your faith?

....

....

....

....

....

....

Take all these responses to God in prayer. Ask Him to help you recognize that your negative thoughts do not come from Him. Ask God to help you replace the negative thoughts with thoughts that represent His love for you. Make a commitment to begin each day in prayer that God will help you replace your negative inner dialog with words that come from Him.

"Claiming God's hope in your life made a difference in your ability to overcome hopelessness and discouragement."

Day Four

I provided four tips for improving your self-talk and overcoming your discouragement. These are practical tips that can make you more aware of just how much of your inner dialog is negative. Today, and at least for the rest of this week, use at least one of these tips as a test to see if you have a habit of negative self-talk. Did you know that negative self-talk can become such a habit that you may not even be aware of it? Give God the next few days to show you what your inner dialog is like.

Reconnect with God: We've already established that negative self-talk can make it difficult to connect with God. To find out how much negative self-talk is a part of your daily life, use one or more of these practical steps:

1. Negative self-talk can devalue God's work in your life. When you say negative things to yourself, stop and replace the negative words with positive words. Speak good over yourself.
2. Place a rubber band on your wrist. Whenever you speak or think a negative thought, pop the rubber band hard enough to sting. At the end of the day, reflect on the number of times you've acknowledged the negativity in your speech and thoughts about yourself.
3. Choose a couple of positive power statements that you can use personally to combat negative self-talk. Here are several statements of affirmation to choose from if you don't know one:

Deuteronomy 20:4	Romans 8:28
Deuteronomy 31:6	Romans 8:31
Psalm 20:4	2 Corinthians 5:17
Psalm 71:17	Philippians 1:6
Psalm 91:4	Philippians 4:6–8
Psalm 139:13–14	2 Timothy 1:7
Jeremiah 29:11	2 Peter 1:3
Mark 11:24	

4. Implement the *Enjoy Today Own Tomorrow* Power Building Phrase Cards to help you stomp out negative self-talk.

Which of these seem most helpful to you? Which of these are habits that you can build into your daily life? Make your decision and remember that this is only a short-term commitment at this time. You are starting this process to determine whether negative self-talk is an issue you need to face.

Realign your heart: Circle your choice(s) above or write them in your journal, then hold yourself accountable by reading the statements, reflecting on them, praying through them, and documenting your progress in your journal.

Use these journal entries as a time to realign your heart to God. Understand that if negative self-talk has become a habit in your life, it will take work on your part to overcome it.

Reactivate your faith: While this testing can take only a few days, it will require a long-term commitment to replace the negative self-talk with uplifting, powerful, self-affirming messages. Your goal is to work to realign your heart with God's so that His words, His affirmations, and His love replaces your negative self-talk.

Read Genesis 1:27–31 below and underline the words that describe how God views mankind as His creation masterpiece. Then, read Ephesians 2:10 in several translations. You'll see words like *handiwork*, *masterpiece*, and *His creation*. You are God's masterpiece—the only part of His creation that He deemed "very good." When you see yourself as less than that, you devalue what He sees as "very good" and as His best creative work. Allow that thought to lead you into prayer before the One who created you, redeemed you, and loves you.

So God created man in His own image; in the image of God He created him; male and female He created them. Then God blessed them, and God said to them, "Be fruitful and multiply; fill the earth and subdue it; have dominion over the fish of the sea, over the birds of the air, and over every living thing that moves on the earth."

And God said, "See, I have given you every herb that yields seed which is on the face of all the earth, and every tree whose fruit yields seed; to you it shall be for food. Also, to every beast of the earth, to every bird of the air, and to everything that creeps on the earth, in which there is life, I have given every green herb for food"; and it was so. Then God saw everything that He had made, and indeed it was very good. So the evening and the morning were the sixth day. (NKJV)

"You are God's masterpiece—the only part of His creation that He deemed 'very good.'"

Day Five

*A*nother obstacle to overcome when you've been hurt by someone is the ability to trust again. I asked, "How do you trust others after being wounded by someone you love?" (*Enjoy Today Own Tomorrow*). Trusting someone who has injured you is hard—sometimes almost impossibly so.

One research study determined that the key to knowing who can be trusted is whether or not they tend to feel guilty. That tendency is called being guilt-prone. I stated that being guilt-prone "anticipates wrongdoing, which keeps the person from making the mistake in the first place." Those who are extremely guilt-prone will avoid doing something untrustworthy. That information can help you reconnect with God.

Reconnect with God: I explained that the study mentioned above "suggests that trustworthiness comes from one's own belief as to how personally responsible they are for their own behavior." That explanation reminds us that we can choose to trust someone who has hurt us because we can trust God.

God is completely trustworthy. What does that mean you can trust Him for?

. . . .

. . . .

. . . .

. . . .

. . . .

The short answer to the question above is "everything"! You can trust God implicitly. Break down God's trustworthiness and you'll see that His trustworthiness is greater than the sum of its parts. Consider the validity of these statements:

➤ God is trustworthy because He is the Creator who designed the entire world and mankind for it.
➤ God is trustworthy because His promises are always kept.
➤ God is trustworthy because He has never lied. He is truth; He cannot be less than truthful.

Compare those statements to the trustworthiness of someone who hurt you. There's no way that any person can live up to those statements. But God can!

Realign your heart: God wants only the best for you and His word is full of promises of His desires for you. For example:

➤ "And we know that in all things God works for the good of those who love him, who have been called according to his purpose."—Romans 8:28
➤ "For no matter how many promises God has made, they are 'Yes' in Christ. And so through him the 'Amen' is spoken by us to the glory of God."—2 Corinthians 1:20
➤ "But according to His promise we are waiting for new heavens and a new earth in which righteousness dwells."—2 Peter 3:13 ESV

How have you seen God's promises fulfilled in your life? List those in your journal and then read the complete list several times aloud. How has God proved His trustworthiness to you?

Reactivate your faith: You've probably already recognized that the process of healing—of learning to forgive those who have hurt you, of establishing positive self-talk that reflects God's love for you, and of being able to trust others because you can trust God—is not a quick fix. It takes time to get past the hurt. It takes spiritual maturity to be ready to forgive someone who has hurt you deeply. It takes effort to work through the steps to bring you to a place of healing and recovery.

Yet, God's healing power is ready for you. He is waiting for you to call upon His power, His wisdom, His comfort, and His healing.

Years ago, a mentor of mine told me she had talked to her father about a big career move but was concerned because of her already advanced age. Her father asked her how old she would be then if she didn't make the decision. Wise words! Healing will take time, but if you don't start, you'll never heal. Wherever you are in this process, turn that over to God now and ask Him to guide you in the process of becoming whole before Him.

"We can choose to trust someone who has hurt us because we can trust God."

Weekend Reflection

This has possibly been another tough week emotionally. You've revisited hurt and pain that you've probably tried to cover up and forget. You've looked at what it will take emotionally and spiritually to forgive the one who caused that hurt and pain. You've considered the impact of that hurt on your life through discouragement and defeat. And, you've begun to consider what it would be like to again be able to trust those who have hurt you.

You've also been encouraged to memorize scripture verses, spend time in studying God's Word, and journal. It's been a lot. So, over the weekend, spend time resting in the Lord. Listen to praise and worship music. Spend time with those who matter the most to you. And, then, when you are relaxed and rested, journal about this week's experiences with these prompts:

What have you learned about your relationship with God right now?

What feelings have you experienced during this process?

· ·

· ·

· ·

· ·

· ·

What do you want your relationship with God to be like?

· ·

· ·

· ·

· ·

· ·

What steps are you prepared to take to grow in your relationship with God?

· ·

· ·

· ·

· ·

· ·

WEEKEND Meditation from *Enjoy Today, Own Tomorrow* Promise Cards

THOUGH I AM SURROUNDED BY TROUBLES,
  you will protect me from the anger of my enemies.
You reach out your hand,
  and the power of your right hand saves me.

Psalm 138:7 (NLT)

Take your time with journaling, meditation, and prayer before you move into week 4. Allow God to speak to you about your relationship with Him and His desires for you.

Week 4

RECONNECT WITH GOD WHEN THE PEOPLE OF THE CHURCH HURT YOU

From My Heart to Yours

Dearest sister, I know how hard it is when someone in the church hurts us. I am so thankful that we are on this journey together so that we can heal and move on with our lives. Healing begins when we have been able to forgive those who should have known better than to break our hearts.

Let Us Pray

Dear God, this is so hard. Please help us as we attempt to pray for our enemies. Help us, God, to realize that these other believers are just people who are also wounded and broken, just like us. Lord, help us to overcome rejection and betrayal, and help us draw closer to you.

Lord, help us understand how the enemy enjoys seeing us hurt and fallen from the community of other believers. Lord, we speak and trust your own words that no weapon formed against us will prosper. God, we know and believe that you will mend our broken hearts and help us trust other believers again.

In Jesus's name, amen!

Introduction

Sometimes, we can be most hurt by people in the church—the one place where we should be safe. In *Enjoy Today Own Tomorrow*, I described the possibilities: "Maybe someone in church said hurtful things to you. Maybe members of the church have damaged you through sexual or verbal abuse, judgment, or rejection. Or possibly, fellow believers have hurt you emotionally." Do these descriptors resonate with you? Do they remind you of times when you've been hurt by people you expected better of?

We expect the people of Christ to be like Him. Sadly, Christians are flawed individuals and they have the potential to be very unChristlike.

This week, we'll look at the impact of the hurt that church members can cause us. And, we'll look at how to move beyond that pain.

Day One

$\mathcal{T}$here are three steps you can take to begin to deal with the pain you've experienced through people in the church. Like we've seen in the chapters we've studied already, getting beyond this hurt is possible, but it is up to us to do the work to make that happen.

Reconnect with God: Consider the first step in healing the wounds caused within the church:

Step 1: Realize that people are just people. I emphasized, "The church is filled with folks who are flawed and full of sin. No one can be excluded."

Start by acknowledging your own sin as it is displayed in the church. Here are a few examples:

➢ Have you judged the actions of others with a higher standard than you use in your own life?
➢ Do you gossip or share things that have been told to you in private?
➢ Do the sins of others make you feel better about your own sins?
➢ Have you said things that have hurt or wounded others?

If you're honest with yourself, you probably feel a little guilty right now. That's what sin does to us. It makes us defensive, and it can make us look for somewhere else to put the blame.

Now, think of how you've been hurt by someone in the church. Recall the details. Think of how you've related to that person before he or she wounded you. Begin to recognize that what was said or done was because of the sin. I wrote, "That does not justify the pain caused by others, but it certainly makes it bearable, and perhaps more reasonable, to walk down the path of learning how to overcome from these wounds."

Realign your heart: The next step requires you to get honest and transparent with yourself.

Step 2: Recognize and identify the pain you are experiencing. I wrote, "We must turn our focus away from people and lean into God like never before. We must unpack all of the raw emotions, be truthful with God, and lay them at His feet."

Look at these possible emotions you could be experiencing and circle those that are present in your life right now. Add others if needed.

Anger	Dismissed	Out-of-control
Chaos	Embarrassment	Pain
Depressed	Emotional	Pessimistic
Disappointment	Isolation	Rejection
Discouraged	Loneliness	Sadness

Lay these open before God. Then, read the verse below several times:

THE LORD HIMSELF GOES BEFORE YOU AND WILL BE WITH YOU; HE WILL NEVER LEAVE YOU NOR FORSAKE YOU. DO NOT BE AFRAID; DO NOT BE DISCOURAGED.

Deuteronomy 31:8

This verse gives comfort for those who are discouraged, hurt, and struggling with loneliness. Use a Bible concordance to search for other verses that give hope and comfort for the emotions you've marked above. Write these in your journal and read them daily as you seek God's comfort and direction in this time.

Reactivate your faith: Step three requires you to make a choice in your relationship with God.

Step 3: Let go of any blame you have placed on God. God is as disappointed as you are that one of His people caused you pain. In fact, God hurts with you. The fault is not His.

Focus the next minutes on the character of God. Search a Bible concordance or online for His character. Some of the characteristics you'll find include His love and compassion, His mercy, and His forgiveness. Record your findings in your journal.

Pray over these characteristics, putting each one in a sentence that connects you to the aspects of God's character, such as:

"GOD, YOU LOVE ME SO DEEPLY THAT YOU HURT WITH ME."
"God, You hurt with me when I cry."
"God, You get disappointed when we believers hurt others."

These steps can move you to a place of allowing God to heal the hurt and pain that's been caused by people in the church.

"Getting beyond this hurt is possible, but it is up to us to do the work to make that happen."

Day Two

*W*e've already worked through the importance of granting forgiveness to those who've hurt you. Granting forgiveness is necessary for you to be able to heal. And in the case of someone who has been hurt sexually or abused verbally, granting forgiveness is impossible without God's help. The greatest resource for that is prayer.

Reconnect with God: I wrote, "We must incorporate prayer into the process of letting go of the deeds of our offenders. . . . Prayer absolutely puts the devil's plans into total defeat. The devil loves it when we hurt each other. He celebrates when God's children create chaos. Conflict gives us all the justification we need to quit, give up, or walk away from any form of faith pursuits."

Conflict of any kind in the church hurts believers, hurts the local church of Christ, and presents a contradictory message to the world. How can we as believers claim the love of Christ when we allow conflict and disunity within the church—even if that disunity comes from one believer hurting another?

Realign your heart: How then do we pray for our enemies? Isn't it sad to think of another believer as an enemy? Yet, anyone who creates disunity in the church becomes an enemy to it. I provided three steps:

1. *Pray that your enemy finds the love of God and has a change of heart.* Only God can turn hearts from evil to good.
2. *Ask God to protect others from this person or persons, so that more hurt will be prevented.*
3. *Pray for mercy for those who hurt us.*

These requests may seem impossible. Yet, Jesus, after been beaten and crucified on the Cross, asked God to forgive those who hurt Him, even to the point of His own death.

Reactivate your faith: None of this is easy, but it is possible through the Holy Spirit. My words can be used as your prayer right now. Cling to these truths about God, which have been edited to be personal statements:

IN MY WEAKEST STATE, GOD IS MY STRENGTH.
When I am hopeless, God steps in and gives me hope.
When my shattered heart is in a million pieces, His touch brings my heart comfort, and the mosaic of my heart take a beautiful shape.
When I feel powerless and as though I can't go on, in the mean times of life, God resurrects me with the confidence of knowing He loves me intimately and that everything will turn out all right.

"Granting forgiveness is necessary for you to be able to heal. The greatest resource for that is prayer."

Day Three

I pointed out that "the healing process can be challenging. The Christian church is meant to be our refuge, a safe place and a gathering of Christ followers who love the Lord and supposedly live that out in their daily walk. But God's house, the corporate church, is filled with hurting people. How we handle those hurts is essential to our living out the life we love."

The reality is that many people run away from the church when they are hurt or wounded by it. Church rolls are evidence of the number of people who never moved their membership to another church but have just stopped attending. Many of them have a story of what someone said or did that hurt them so profoundly that they just couldn't go back. Satan rejoices in those moments. As John 10:10 states, "The thief comes only to steal and kill and destroy."

The church of Christ is God's gift to believers. Yet, disunity hurts the work of the church. How, then, should the church confront divisive issues and behavior?

Reconnect with God: Based on your knowledge, what do you see as divisive issues and behavior within the church? List these below:

. . . .

. . . .

. . . .

. . . .

. . . .

Did you include sexual abuse or the presence of sexual predators? Sexual sin that is not confronted reflects an unhealthy culture within the church that impacts everyone in it. The church has an obligation to deal with things that are ungodly within the church. Too often, the church tries to hide terrible sin rather than confess it before the world.

Confronting horrific sin within the church allows healing to take place. How have you seen the church hold people accountable?

Realign your heart: Another issue within the church is what I referred to as "trial-and-jury atmosphere." I explained, "I'll admit, it sounds a little crazy. The very people who are tasked to love as Christ loves us—unconditionally—have now placed a human judgment upon us. If we have tattoos, radical hairstyles, are divorced, or struggling with any type of sin in our lives, we may come under the microscope."

Consider this statement: "The very community Jesus set up (and died for) so that the church could become the physician to the broken world has now wounded others through individuals of the church who are sick as well." What will it take for the church to heal itself so it can minister to our broken world?

Reactivate your faith: I make a powerful statement about how the church's shortcomings can affect us: "Many times, in these situations, a fallout symptom is that we start to question whether or not we are worthy of God's love. We can be too hard on ourselves, either by casting doubt or attempting to measure our value and worth through the lens of a negative experience."

Close this time in prayer:

➤ Ask God to search your heart, motives, and lifestyle and reveal to you what He finds lacking.
➤ Ask God for His forgiveness, grace, and mercy for these issues.
➤ Ask God to help you accept His forgiveness so you can forgive yourself.

"But God's house, the corporate church, is filled with hurting people. How we handle those hurts is essential to our living out the life we love."

Day Four

One result of being hurt by someone in the church is feeling rejected. I wrote, "Sometimes other Christians hurt us by making us feel as though we don't belong, another powerful weapon the enemy uses to take us away from the church." How can you fight the feelings of rejection?

Reconnect with God: Possibly the best place to start in dealing with rejection is to identify whether you are struggling with rejection. Rejection has been defined as being cast away, thrown away, or discarded. Characteristics of feeling rejected include:

Grief	Sadness
Isolation	Shame
Loneliness	Social anxiety

Circle those you are experiencing (or have experienced in the past) because of feeling rejected. How can these feelings make it difficult to reconnect your heart with God's?

. . . .

. . . .

. . . .

. . . .

. . . .

These feelings can cause you to build emotional walls so others can't hurt you again. When those emotional walls are built against someone in the church, the walls can prevent you from building healthy relationships with others and can even damage your trust in God.

Do you see these emotional walls built in your life? If so, how have they impacted your relationship with others in the church and with God?

....

....

....

....

....

....

Realign your heart: We've all been rejected at times in our lives. Experiencing rejection, though, can bring us back to God and allow Him to speak directly to the way we live our lives. I used the example of Sandy's rejection by church leadership to show that sometimes the church rejects us personally and not because of a sin in our lives. Rejection like that could be based on our race, our gender, or things like a failure in a marriage. I even read about a church that dismissed members if they didn't vote the way the pastor wanted.

Have you seen or experienced this kind of rejection in the church? Was God glorified in the process? Have you felt the need to change churches because of some kind of prejudiced behavior? How did God work in that process?

Reactivate your faith: I emphasized that, "As we battle against rejection, we can never forget whose we are or who we are." Read Galatians 4:4–5. Then, pray through these statements:

> ➢ I am one of God's own children, and He hand-made me.
> ➢ God designed me to fulfill His plan in my life.

➢ I can't allow the perceptions of others to let me lose sight of who I am in Christ.
➢ I am a child of God.

"Experiencing rejection, though, can bring us back to God and allow Him to speak directly to the way we live our lives."

Day Five

*Y*ou've overviewed how you can be hurt or wounded by people in the church. You've considered steps to take to begin healing, and you've evaluated how rejection has made you feel. There's one overarching truth throughout this chapter for you to focus on—reconnecting with God through these wounds is the only way to heal. I wrote, "No matter how deep the hurt, God is the answer."

Reconnect with God: You've been asked to reflect on your feelings of hurt and rejection throughout this week. Sadly, being emotionally hurt by people you've trusted can impact your ability to trust God. As you seek to reconnect with God today, respond to the following questions:

What is your faith foundation built upon? Is it the people in the church, the ministers in the church, the word of God, or your relationship with Christ?

....

....

....

....

....

....

Has your faith given you hope while you've dealt with these feelings? Why?

. . . .

. . . .

. . . .

. . . .

. . . .

. . . .

Read Psalm 34:18. How have you seen God draw near to you during this time? Have you accepted His nearness to you? Why?

. . . .

. . . .

. . . .

. . . .

. . . .

Realign your heart: I described *hope* as "another great healing balm for our broken hearts." While we usually think of the word *hope* as something we want to happen, the word means something totally different in the Bible. In scripture, *hope* is the expectation of what God has promised to do.

Read Psalm 62:5: "For God alone, O my soul, wait in silence, for my hope is from him" (ESV). Why can you depend upon God's hope?

. . . .

. . . .

. . . .

. . . .

. . . .

. . . .

Hebrews 11:1 explains the relationship between *faith* and *hope*: "Now faith is confidence in what we hope for and assurance about what we do not see." I explained that having hope in the Lord allowed me to let Him teach me even in difficult times. I wrote, "I have found that when I am in my most desperate places, I hear God better than ever. During these times, God reveals crucial comfort, revelation, and peace that is often not as clear to me when life is going smoothly."

What have you learned from God during these difficult times we've looked at this week?

. . . .

. . . .

. . . .

. . . .

. . . .

. . . .

Reactivate your faith: Close this session by acknowledging your hope in the Lord. Then, close with praying these words I wrote to close the chapter:

As we continue to keep our minds and hearts focused on God meeting us wherever we are with open arms and a love that heals all of our wounds, then we can find the strength to move forward. God never promised us that life would be without pain and suffering, but He did promise He would always be with us every step of the way. God's love and justice will give us complete vindication and an eventual sweet victory, which enables us to enjoy today and own tomorrow right now. (59)

"Reconnecting with God through these wounds is the only way to heal."

Weekend Reflection

Has this been a tough week emotionally? If you've been hurt through the church, you may have some deep wounds that are, as yet, still raw. This weekend, spend time reflecting on where you are with God. Are you open to His drawing near to you? Have you built up emotional walls to protect you that keep Him away? Are you clinging to the hope you have in Christ?

When you are relaxed and rested, journal about this week's experiences with these prompts:

What have your learned about your relationship with God right now?

. . . .

. . . .

. . . .

. . . .

. . . .

. . . .

What feelings have you experienced during this process?

What do you want your relationship with God to be like?

What steps are you prepared to take to grow in your relationship with God?

WEEKEND Meditation from *Enjoy Today, Own Tomorrow* Promise Cards

WHEN YOU GO THROUGH DEEP WATERS,
  I will be with you.
When you go through rivers of difficulty,
  you will not drown.
When you walk through the fire of oppression,
  you will not be burned up;
  the flames will not consume you.

Isaiah 43:2 NLT

Take your time with journaling, meditation, and prayer before you move into week 5. Allow God to speak to you about your relationship with Him and His desires for you.

Week 5

REALIGNING BEGINS WITH YOUR HEART

From My Heart to Yours

Dearest sister, we have come so far in this healing journey together. I pray this is the week in which you will see that joy, hope, and happiness can be ours as we realign our hearts to God.

Let Us Pray

Dear Father, help us in every way to find you in the center of our daily lives. Help us to align our hearts with yours so that we find spiritual healing. We know that the healing power is found only in you, Lord.

Allow us to unpack all the terrible emotions that are a result of devastating pains we have experienced. Lord, perform spiritual heart surgery on us this week as you cut away the calloused layers of our hearts, only to make more room for your love, healing, and comfort. We know it is only you that has the power to transform our lives.

Lord, help us unplug from the noisy world and crawl into your quiet presence, so that we can rest in your providence and protection.

In Jesus's name, amen!

Introduction

In my book, I pointed out that spiritual alignment is essential in being able to enjoy today and own tomorrow. However, I also pointed out that spiritual alignment can be difficult after we have been through tough times. I wrote, "Chaos and confusion often hover over us while we face grief and pain. We long to know how we will get through. The act of picking up the pieces of our lives after we have been tossed and emotionally torn to pieces can be overwhelming."

Have you wondered if you'll ever find joy, hope, and happiness again? Have you questioned if you'll be able to move beyond all you've gone through? This week, you'll have the chance to consider how to answer both of these questions.

Day One

When we talk about spiritual concepts, it's always best to start by understanding what the concepts are about. It's one thing to define a word like *alignment*, and another to define the concept of *spiritual alignment*.

Think of ways you've used the concept of alignment. You've probably had your tires re-aligned, which means the tires are adjusted to make sure they work efficiently together. If you've broken a bone, you've had a doctor realign the bone so it will heal properly. Alignment has to do with getting things to where they are supposed to be for maximum efficiency. Alignment can be defined as being arranged in a line or in proper position.

Reconnect with God: *Spiritual alignment* means being aligned properly—being in the right position—with God. I explained the need for spiritual alignment this way: "Some of us are like a set of tires that are in desperate need of truing up. Our hearts have been shattered and our tread is almost nonexistent. Life has been bumpy, and we have been rigorously shaken."

Using the tire analogy, evaluate your own spiritual alignment. Which of these terms best describes your relationship with God:

Life is straight and strong.	Life is veering off the road.
Life is smooth.	Life is bumpy.
Life is under control.	Life is spiraling out of control.
Life is moving like a pleasant drive.	Life seems to be racing toward a disaster.

Obviously, the statements on the left describe a life aligned with God, and the statements on the right describe a life that needs to be realigned with Him. I explained, "Alignment is the act of coming into agreement with God—physically, emotionally, spiritually—seeking

His best for our lives and surrendering our broken hearts." What difference would it make in your life if you became realigned and reconnected to God?

Realign your heart: We began this discussion with the challenge of realigning our hearts with God. The term *heart* is another word that needs defining from a biblical perspective. We think of our hearts as the organ that pumps the blood through our bodies and gives us life. The reality is that if our heart quits beating, we die. Period.

In the Bible, the term *heart* also speaks to life, but it points to our spiritual lives rather than our physical lives. If our spiritual hearts become disconnected from God's heart, we die spiritually. Period. We cannot stay alive in God if our hearts are dead to Him.

Compare the characteristics of God's heart to human hearts that are not aligned with His:

GOD'S HEART	HUMAN HEARTS WITHOUT GOD
God's heart is pure.	Human hearts are evil and self-focused.
God's heart is compassionate.	Human hearts focus on evil, immorality, and sin.

The heart is mentioned over a thousand times in the Bible. That's an indication of just how important our *spiritual heart* is.

Reactivate your faith: God knows the precise condition of your heart. There are no secrets, no hidden things, in your life that He doesn't already know. According to Proverbs 23:7, "For as [man] thinks in his heart, so is he" (NKJV). I wrote, "Our hearts literally define our thoughts, motivations, and actions. The contents make up who we are, what we do with our lives, and how we act."

You've had a chance to consider the state of your spiritual heart. Does your heart need realigning to be like His? Are there things in your life that have caused you to veer away from Him? Confess those things to the Lord in prayer. Then, claim God's promise in Ezekiel 36:26–27: "I will take away your stubborn heart and give you a new heart and a desire to be faithful. You will have only pure thoughts, because I will put my Spirit in you and make you eager to obey my laws and teachings" (CEV).

"Alignment is the act of coming into agreement with God—physically, emotionally, spiritually—seeking His best for our lives and surrendering our broken hearts."

Day Two

*I*n chapter 2, we focused on the fact that it was not in God's plan that humankind would suffer. Think about how the garden of Eden is described in Genesis. It was a place of perfect beauty, perfect unity in creation, and perfect peace. It lacked nothing. Yet, evil entered into the garden and Adam and Eve both succumbed to it. They had everything, but they were made to feel like something was missing. Their sinful desires opened up sickness, death, betrayal, rejection, and disobedience to God.

Adam and Eve's struggle with sin became our struggle. Their embracing of evil opened us up to the pull of evil in our lives. And Satan takes full advantage of those openings. I wrote, "Some of Satan's attacks are so violent and strong they shatter our hearts. Many of us want to run from God. We often try to find worldly ways to deal with our pain. This is when we need God the most." Only God can bring healing.

Reconnect with God: While we cannot fix our broken hearts, God can. I described God as "the Master Heart Surgeon" and said that He alone is the spiritual heart surgeon. "If we can literally put our hearts into a man or woman's hands—then why would we fail to put our trust in God's hands in the midst of trials that leave us spiritually brokenhearted?"

Has anything stopped you from turning to God for healing? If so, what?

Why have you allowed those reasons to keep you from leaning on God?

. . . .

. . . .

. . . .

. . . .

. . . .

. . . .

Realign your heart: I described Satan's strategy to keep us from allowing God to heal us is to keep his attacks coming. I asked, "Have you noticed how things seem to happen in multiples—the car breaks down, and before it is fixed, one of the kids is sick, only to be quickly followed by a layoff? We can consistently feel hopeless, angry, depressed, and more" (65). These attacks can paralyze us emotionally and spiritually.

Is your spiritual life losing ground to tests, trials, and temptations? Is it possible that Satan is bringing attack upon attack on your life and your family?

. . . .

. . . .

. . . .

. . . .

. . . .

. . . .

If you answered yes to the questions above, prayerfully consider why you might be under attack. Is Satan's attack keeping you from being who God called you to be or doing what God called you to do?

. . . .

. . . .

. . . .

. . . .

. . . .

. . . .

Reactivate your faith: There's only one way to find spiritual healing. That's through the healing power of God. There's only one way to fight Satan's attacks on your life. That's through the healing power of God and the redemptive work of Christ.

The pattern of these two statements must not be missed. Our healing comes only through God. We cannot do it ourselves. We cannot do it with the help of others, no matter how well-intentioned they are. We cannot do it. Only God can bring that healing.

Read Luke 4:18 and then pray for God to begin to heal your heart, to strengthen your resistance to Satan, and to empower you to realign your heart to His.

"While we cannot fix our broken hearts, God can."

Day Three

I acknowledge that trusting God when our hearts are broken can be difficult. I wrote, "We may have to struggle to deepen our belief in who God is. We must learn to trust God with every detail of our lives—good and bad. Trust is an action that our hearts must risk."

The question for today is, Are you ready to trust God with every detail of your life? If you answered yes, then what are you willing to do to make that happen?

Reconnect with God: So, how then do you go about realigning your heart with God and His will for you? I suggest you begin by assessing where you are in this moment. Ask yourself: *Is my heart full of anger? Disappointment? Pain? Sorrow? Bitterness? Unbelief? Fear?*

Are these emotional burdens taking up space in your heart? Do they take up so much space that there's no room for God? If they were removed, what could your spiritual heart look like?

Realign your heart: The emotional and spiritual pain listed above are like cancers to your soul. They must be cut out, just like cancerous tumors are removed, so your heart and soul can begin to heal.

Use this opportunity to begin to excise these negative burdens. In your journaling, list those heavy burdens that your carry. Remember what happened in your life that caused these burdens to settle on you. Think of the things you've tried in order to remove these burdens on your own. Recognize where you have not been successful in reclaiming your life.

. . . .

. . . .

. . . .

. . . .

. . . .

. . . .

Reactivate your faith: Medical research has identified how seriously a broken heart can impact your physical life. They have named it broken heart syndrome or stress cardiomyopathy, and they've found that having an emotionally broken heart can cause long-term damage to the muscle of the heart. Hanging on to deep emotional pain can literally cause you long-term physical damage. Do you need to seek God's healing to realign your heart and reactivate your faith?

Psalm 51:1–12 is a beautiful picture of how God can heal your life. Read these verses aloud as your prayer. Focus on the words of the psalm that describe how God's healing can transform your life. Then, spend time journaling about what your life will be like when you've realigned your heart with His.

"We must learn to trust God with every detail of our lives—good and bad. Trust is an action that our hearts must risk."

Day Four

We've already spent a significant time on prayer—learning ways to pray, learning why prayer is necessary in our lives, and praying specifically for God's guidance in this journey and for His healing in our lives. Prayer is as necessary for Christians as air to breathe is for people. We cannot live spiritually without it. Today, we'll specifically look at how to pray as we realign our hearts with God's.

Reconnect with God: In *Enjoy Today Own Tomorrow*, I pointed out that our regular prayers—"a typical religious prayer recital"—will not be effective in trying to realign our hearts with His. Rather, I described prayer for realignment as trusting God with everything we are feeling—the good, the bad, and the ugly. I wrote, "These prayers are the union between an individual and God. They can even be silent prayers, when we are often truly at a loss for words. We can set our hearts on God and sit silently before Him. All we need are prayers that come straight from the heart. Prayers that come from the excruciating pain felt within."

Use this as a journaling opportunity. Write your prayer that comes from the deepest place in your heart. If you have no words, write: "Lord, I have no words, but I need you." You can destroy your prayer afterward if you don't want anyone to possibly see it. Or, you can let it become part of the process of beginning to learn anew how to pray from the deep hurts you carry.

....

....

....

....

....

....

Realign your heart: Your prayer for realignment should also acknowledge the grief you are experiencing. Grief can come from the loss of someone or something in your life. It can also come from the results of past decisions, for actions that you'd give anything not to have done, and for the person that you've been in the past. Whatever is causing you to grieve must be acknowledged. Embrace the emotions, reflect on the grief, and ask God to help you begin to move past it. Begin to embrace fully God's hope and His unconditional forgiveness that He has granted you.

Reactivate your faith: Prayer that seeks God's heart allows you to develop trust in who He is and who you are in Him. He will strengthen your heart through prayer. He will draw near to you through prayer. He will empower you to face the temptations and trials of the world through prayer. He will take away your unbelief and your fear through prayer.

Yesterday, you prayed through Psalm 51:1–12. Today, go there again, and focus on verses 1–2. Pray these words aloud, confessing your transgressions (something that goes against what God expects), iniquities (immoral or unfair behavior), and sins (disobedience to God) before Him. Then, focus on the words in the psalm that describe who you are in God's forgiveness—your sins have been washed away so that they are no longer, and you've been cleansed internally and restored back to Him. End this session by journaling about the healing available to you that we've talked about in this session.

"Prayer is as necessary for Christians as air to breathe is for people."

Day Five

I introduced the acronym REST (rely every second today on God) at the end of chapter 5 in *Enjoy Today, Own Tomorrow*. I explained, "If we hand over every second and every emotion to God, then we can always rest in Him. In times of despair, finding rest can get complicated. . . . We must be intentional about resting in God."

Think about what it means to you to find rest in your life. Probably you're thinking about times of ease, of comfort, of safety, and of peace. Today, determine what it would be like to REST in God.

Reconnect with God: Psalm 62:1–2 states,

For God alone my soul waits in silence;
  from him comes my salvation.
He alone is my rock and my salvation,
  my fortress; I shall not be greatly shaken (ESV).

These verses give a picture of finding rest in God. Now read this interpretation based on what we've considered this week:

> My soul waits in silence (because I don't have words to bring before Him) for God alone. He sent His Son to bring me salvation. He is my foundation on which I live and the place where I find safety and refuge. Because I can depend upon Him, nothing done by man or Satan can shake my faith.

Contemplate these words. What words or phrases would you change to make this statement yours alone?

. . . .

. . . .

. . . .

. . . .

. . . .

. . . .

Realign your heart: The psalmist wrote, "Be still, and know that I am God" (Psalm 46:10 NKJV). What would it take to be totally still before God?

. . . .

. . . .

. . . .

. . . .

. . . .

Being still includes quieting all the noise around you (phone, internet, computer, TV, radio), and quieting your mind (putting everything that occupies your mind aside). It's definitely easier for some people than for others.

What areas of your life are hard to quiet to be able to come fully into God's presence?

. . . .

. . . .

. . . .

. . . .

. . . .

. . . .

You may have noted a busy life, a full to-do list, the stress of deadlines, a crowded and chaotic household. It's easy to recognize where the external noises come from, but much harder to conquer the noise internally. Write a list of the names of God that are meaningful to you.

. . . .

. . . .

. . . .

. . . .

. . . .

. . . .

If you don't have more than one or two, google names of God online and add them to your list. Use this list of the names of God to help you focus on who He is as you come into His presence.

Reactivate your faith: Coming into the presence of God makes us feel safe. There is nothing He cannot overcome. There is nothing He cannot do. All things are possible in God alone.

Read David's words about God in Psalm 139:1–12. Then, use these words as a guide to describe how God is everywhere you are, such as, "When I am sitting in the car line to pick up my children, you are there!" List as many specific places as you can where God's presence is with you and then thank Him for His presence in your life.

"There is nothing He cannot overcome. There is nothing He cannot do. All things are possible in God alone."

Weekend Reflection

You've spent this week evaluating the condition of your heart. You've taken the first step toward realigning your heart with His. This weekend, as you rest, also REST in the Lord. Begin to pray about what you want your heart to be like. Acknowledge the areas that are ungodly and give those to God. Set aside some time to be still in His presence.

Over the weekend, journal about this week's experiences with these prompts:

What have your learned about your present relationship with God?

. . . .

. . . .

. . . .

. . . .

. . . .

. . . .

What feelings have you experienced during this process?

. . . .

. . . .

. . . .

. . . .

. . . .

What do you want your relationship with God to be like?

. . . .

. . . .

. . . .

. . . .

. . . .

What steps are you prepared to take to grow in your relationship with God?

. . . .

. . . .

. . . .

. . . .

. . . .

WEEKEND Meditation from *Enjoy Today, Own Tomorrow* Declaration Cards

"COME TO ME, ALL OF YOU WHO ARE WEARY AND BURDENED, AND I WILL GIVE YOU REST."

Matthew 11:28

Take your time with journaling, meditation, and prayer before you move into week 6. Allow God to speak to you about your relationship with Him and His desires for you.

Week 6

WHAT SPIRITUAL REALIGNMENT LOOKS LIKE

From My Heart to Yours

Dearest sister, I am so grateful that this week we know that the power of healing can only be found in the presence of God! Now that we have surrendered our hearts, we have a desire to be with God, and we are continually digging deeper daily as we recognize and acknowledge Him. As we do these actions, we discover that God cares for us uniquely and guides our every step. Then, we can hear His voice when we pursue His presence. We will see our lives spiritually aligning with His daily.

Let Us Pray

Dear God, please help us as we come to you with the eyes of our hearts wide open. Lord, reveal to us who you are. Help us be in your presence more, praise you more, pray more often, and worship who you are. Lord, we desire to be more intentional with you and to spiritually realign our lives and live in an intimate relationship with you.

In Jesus's name, amen!

Introduction

In *Enjoy Today Own Tomorrow*, I explained that after surrendering our hearts to God, "The next step is aligning our lives spiritually, following the path He laid down for us before we were even born. We can choose to build up our core foundation from the things He intended for us—including our dreams and destinies." To do this successfully requires pursuing God with all that we are.

Imagine how your life could transform if you made pursuing God your priority. Pursuing God passionately will gradually begin to change who you are, reshaping you through things that are new and chosen. And the journey will lead you to true healing.

I emphasize that "everything we could want or need to enjoy today, and own tomorrow is found in the presence of God." Whether we need to be raised from the pit of despair, healed of our wounds, or lacking anything in our lives, we can find what we need in His presence, His healing, and His accessibility. This week, begin that journey by opening the eyes of your heart to see all things new in Him.

Day One

I stated, "Pursuing God begins with intentional living. It starts with a plan and a purpose to be with God." That means there is a process allowing God to change you into the person He created you to be. This process—surrendering our hearts to Him, pursuing Him, and desiring Him with all that we are—creates fertile ground in which He can work.

Reconnect with God: Last week, we discussed *spiritual alignment*. With that foundation, it's easy to see how pursuing God with all that we are can lead us to become spiritually aligned with God. When we surrender everything to God, we can begin to recognize His presence. And, when you discover truly being in the presence of our holy Lord, you'll realize that you cannot survive without it.

Describe a life that has been fully surrendered to God, a life that has learned to live in and depend upon the presence of God.

. . . .

. . . .

. . . .

. . . .

. . . .

. . . .

Did your description come from the example of someone you know or something you've read in scripture? Or, did it come from the deepest desire of your heart? What would you have to do to claim that kind of life for yourself?

....

....

....

....

....

....

Realign your heart: I wrote, "We may rarely be challenged or exposed to the idea of seeking God in a deeper way. Yet this is God's one desire—to be in a meaningful relationship with all of us. Yes, God is omnipresent. He is always around us every second of every day. . . . The only thing we have to do in response is to be intentional in recognizing and acknowledging Him in our pursuit every day."

First Chronicles 28:9 gives a beautiful description of what pursuing God looks like:

> And you, my son Solomon, acknowledge the God of your father, and serve him with wholehearted devotion and with a willing mind, for the LORD searches every heart and understands every desire and every thought. If you seek him, he will be found by you; but if you forsake him, he will reject you forever.

Circle each of the verbs in this verse that are actions of pursuing God. Next, underline each of the descriptive phrases that describe your attitude and desire in those actions. Finally, draw a rectangle around the results you'll experience from pursuing God.

This powerful verse makes it clear what is required in pursuing God—"if you seek him, he will be found." It also presents what is lost if we don't—"if you forsake him, he will reject you forever."

Reactivate your faith: God cares about every aspect of our lives. What happens to you matters to Him. The choices you make matter to Him. The pain you struggle under matters to Him. Paul encouraged his young protégé Timothy with these words: "But you, man of God, flee from all this, and pursue righteousness, godliness, faith, love, endurance and gentleness" (1 Timothy 6:11).

Ask God to teach you to pursue His righteousness and godliness, to strengthen your faith, to teach you to love like Jesus loves, and to help you discover the work that endurance and gentleness can do in your life.

"Pursuing God begins with intentional living. It starts with a plan and a purpose to be with God."

Day Two

Living in the presence of God will begin to change not only how you understand God but how you see yourself as well. Think back over the creation account (or read Genesis 1 if you want to examine the details). Find answers to these questions:

➢ Why did God create the world?
➢ For whom did God create the world?
➢ What was God's greatest accomplishment in His creation, the thing that He was most pleased with?
➢ How does God feel about His creation now?

Here's what the Bible says about these:

➢ God created the world in order to have an intimate relationship with mankind.
➢ God created the world for mankind.
➢ When God created mankind in His image, He said that it was "very good."
➢ God loves His created world and *everything* in it as much today as He did in its beginning.

Are these questions and answers redundant? Not exactly. Yes, everything God did was for mankind. Yes, God created us in His image. Yes, God continues to love us deeply and deeply desires to be in relationship with us. The answers aren't redundant; they are progressive and show the beautiful relationship that God desires to have with us.

Reconnect with God: Our deepest desire should be to come into the presence of God in an intimate relationship with Him. But, how do we do that? In *Enjoy Today, Own Tomorrow*, I provided three practical actions that can bring us closer to Him.

Action 1: Create a special place to come into God's presence.

If you saw the movie *War Room*, you saw a wonderful example of this. The main character cleaned out her closet in order to find a place to focus her attention on God. When she began, she wasn't sure what to do. But, by the middle of the movie, the walls of her closet were covered with praises and prayers.

A special place helps you focus more quickly and clearly because you'll have fewer distractions. Do you have a special place already? If you wanted to create a space, where would you do that?

. . . .

. . . .

. . . .

. . . .

. . . .

. . . .

Routine of place can help you focus immediately on your time with God. Routine prayer prompts can help as well. I always begin our time with this question: "God, what do you need me to do for you today?" It doesn't matter where that special place is—for me it's in my bed before I open my eyes—as long as you are consistent with your time there.

Realign your heart: A special place is a wonderful beginning. Sometimes, however, you can do everything right—consistent place, consistent time, consistent prayer—and feel like you're not where you want to be with God. The next action can help that.

Action 2: Come into God's presence through His words in scripture.

I described God's Word as His "super power for our lives." I explained, "The Word of God supplies power during our personal time with Him. This is when God speaks to us in His own language. The greatest supernatural element to this is the fact that the Word, written in our Bibles, is still living, breathing, and just as valid as it was the day it was written or spoken."

Have you tried reading God's Word aloud as a part of your time with Him? Read Psalm 5 aloud now. Listen to the cadence of the words. Hear the words as God hears them. Recognize where you fit into the words of the psalm. Listen for how God's voice is plainly heard, even when the words are written to Him. There is no substitute for the power of hearing God through His Word.

Reactivate your faith: Coming to God in a special place that's been designated for your time with Him helps you create discipline in your relationship with Him. Listening to His words brings His supernatural power into your relationship. The next action gives you a way to respond to Him.

Action 3: While in the presence of God, journal to create a ledger of your history with Him.

Write your thoughts down. Record what you have prayed for and how you've heard God's voice. Then, write your praises. Think of yourself as a psalmist and allow all that you are feeling toward God to freely flow onto your paper. I emphasized that our thoughts and prayers "truly are a manifestation of what God is telling us. As you receive new revelation about a Scripture passage, make note of what the new thought is. In essence, you are recording your transformation."

"God continues to love us deeply and deeply desires to be in relationship with us."

In my book, I acknowledged, "On occasion, people have asked me about hearing the voice of God. Let me say first that it is a scriptural fact that God speaks to His own children. Why would God create ears if He didn't plan on speaking to us?"

Have you heard the voice of God? Or, are you thinking you might have but you're not sure? Today, as you work through this session, ask God to teach you to recognize His voice when He speaks to you.

Reconnect with God: God speaks to us in a variety of ways. Search these biblical verses and record how God spoke in each. As you work, note if God continues to speak to us that way.

Genesis 3:9–19; 6:13:

1 Kings 19:9–13:

Ezekiel 22:1–3:

Genesis 37:

Acts 10:13–15:

John 20:30–31:

Compare your responses to these:
Genesis 3:9–19; 6:13: God speaks with us personally.
1 Kings 19:9–13: God speaks in a still, small voice.
Ezekiel 22:1–3: God speaks through His prophets.

Genesis 37: God speaks through application drawn from scripture examples.

Acts 10:13–15: God speaks through dreams and visions.

John 20:30–31: God spoke to the writers of the Bible and speaks to us through their writings.

Realign your heart: I tell of times that God speaks to me "through a pressing thought that will not go away" (83). Have you had that experience—someone who keeps coming to mind or an issue that chews on you and you can't put it aside? I describe those nudges as "a tangible way God speaks."

How have you felt God's nudges in such a way that you knew He was speaking to you? How did you respond to those nudges? How did you see God work through those nudges?

. . . .

. . . .

. . . .

. . . .

. . . .

. . . .

I explained, "When we hear and acknowledge the prompting of God, He can use us to move on His behalf. God will press in about things, people, answers to problems, and so much more while we bask in His powerful presence."

Reactivate your faith: I pointed out that "when you hear God pressing anything into your heart, it drowns out the dark and evil voices of the world. You are totally, spiritually aligned."

Ask God to show you who He wants you to pray for. Then, sit in silence and listen to hear God's nudges with names, needs, or issues. List these as they come to you and then ask God to show you how He wants to use you in each situation.

"God will press in about things, people, answers to problems, and so much more while we bask in His powerful presence."

Day Four

We continue to look at how prayer draws us into the presence of God because it is the single most important thing we can do in developing our relationship with Him. I pointed out in *Enjoy Today Own Tomorrow*, "We can take prayer to a new level by inviting heaven to come down to earth on our behalf. Our prayers should be bold and expectant." Today, as you work through this session, ask God to teach you how to pray with boldness and expectancy.

Reconnect with God: What does the word *boldness* mean to you? One online dictionary describes it as "the trait of being willing to undertake things that involve risk or danger." Why is it important that we approach God with boldness?

. . . .

. . . .

. . . .

. . . .

. . . .

. . . .

Read Acts 4:27–31. Why did the believers need to pray for boldness? How did God respond?

. . . .

. . . .

. . . .

. . . .

. . . .

. . . .

Read Acts 4:23–31. Why did Paul need boldness? How did God respond to his need?

. . . .

. . . .

. . . .

. . . .

. . . .

. . . .

I described praying boldly this way: "If we need God to show up and show out, this is the time to ask and expect from God. If we need healing, reconciliation of prodigal relationships, recovery from addiction, or have any particular transforming needs, it is in this deep state of prayer that we can ask with confidence for God to move."

What is keeping you from praying with boldness?

. . . .

. . . .

. . . .

. . . .

. . . .

Realign your heart: I presented Kim Cohen as an example of how God responded to my bold prayers. I concluded, "When we petition our needs boldly, as Kim did, the miracle-working power of God manifests." I then presented three keys for praying boldly:

Key 1: Pray with confidence.

Key 2: Pray in faith.

Key 3: Pray with a heart that is aligned with God's will and providence.

Read Matthew 17:14–20. Which of these keys were present in the disciples' prayers? Which were absent? How did God respond to their prayers?

. . . .

. . . .

. . . .

. . . .

. . . .

Reactivate your faith: These keys are all necessary in praying boldly and hearing God's voice. Praying with these keys can assure you that God will hear your prayers and answer them. However, these keys do not assure you that God will answer the way you want. I wrote, "My caution is that sometimes God answers our heartfelt prayers with a *no* or a *not now*. The confidence to carry on in faith must be based on God's providence and the certainty in who He is, even if the answer is no."

All of us have prayed diligently for things that we didn't see happen in our timing. Think of a couple of those times. Did your confidence in God allow you to accept His answer of *no* or *not now*? Did you ever see His answer in ways you didn't expect?

....

....

....

....

....

....

Close this session in prayer, acknowledging the answered prayers you've seen and celebrating the fact that, even when you don't see what He does, God always answers your prayers.

"We can take prayer to a new level by inviting heaven to come down to earth on our behalf. Our prayers should be bold and expectant."

Day Five

I concluded chapter 6 with examining how the act of praise and worship can bring us into the presence of God. I wrote, "In heaven, there will always be praise and worship because the eternal happy life has been realized. There is no sorrow. When we praise God from earth, in the midst of all of the struggles and darkness of this world, it is a sound that captivates heaven. It catches the ears of the angels because of its unique qualities."

This week, evaluate what worship means to you. Does your worship catch the ears of angels? Why?

. . . .

. . . .

. . . .

. . . .

. . . .

. . . .

Reconnect with God: I compared how God and Satan respond to our worship. I wrote, "When we praise and worship God in the midst of our deepest despair, there is no doubt our voices will echo in the ears of our Heavenly Father. The devil knows this truth. The enemy will do everything in his power to keep us from entering into God's presence with praise and worship."

Describe what the act of worship and praise looks like in your life. Does God hear the echo of your worship? Why?

. . . .

. . . .

. . . .

. . . .

. . . .

Describe what things can intrude upon or interrupt your praise and worship. Do these interruptions keep you from entering the presence of God? Why?

. . . .

. . . .

. . . .

. . . .

. . . .

There's a constant battle within us of who will be in charge of our lives. That battle can be clearly seen when outside things keep us from worshipping God. But we can conquer these intrusions. I wrote, "The devil knows that when we praise God in our greatest weakness, it resounds throughout the heavens to bring us all of God's comfort and life-transforming presence."

Realign your heart: Another element in our praise and worship is showing God our gratitude. I stated, "When we give God our praise, it changes us from the inside out. Our hearts become filled with a thankfulness that changes us within, even if our circumstances have not altered."

Read Hebrews 12:28–29 in a couple of translations. Focus on these words: "Therefore, since we are receiving a kingdom that cannot be shaken, let us be thankful, and so worship God acceptably with reverence and awe" (v. 28).

Our thankfulness should come from two facts. First, God is unshakeable and unchanging. He alone is worthy of our worship. We can be thankful for who God is and for what He has done for us. Second, being thankful in worship is about what He has done for us that has changed and transformed our lives—He has extended His grace to us.

How can holding on to these facts impact the way you enter His presence in worship?

. . . .

. . . .

. . . .

. . . .

. . . .

. . . .

Reactivate your faith: I stressed that our praise and worship can strengthen us to face each day. I also stated that we can become weary, which opens us up to discouragement. But, "The presence of God, along with our praise and worship, edifies our souls" (88). As you close this session in prayer, use these prayer prompts to guide you:

➢ Focus on God's goodness and His sovereignty.
➢ Focus on God's greatness.

➢ Acknowledge that you choose to lean on God's strength, regardless of what you are dealing with in your life.

➢ Ask God to help you depend upon Him more as you grow in your relationship with Him.

"The presence of God, along with our praise and worship, edifies our souls."

Weekend Reflection

This week, you've spent time considering what spiritual realignment looks like when you pursue God intentionally. You've considered what it means to come into the presence of the Holy God. You've also looked at how God can speak to you when you come before Him in prayer, worship, and praise. This weekend, spend time with God. Become more intentional about having private times of praise and worship. Spend time in stillness, listening for His voice and His promptings.

Over the weekend, journal about this week's experiences with these prompts:

What have your learned about your relationship with God right now?

. . . .

. . . .

. . . .

. . . .

. . . .

. . . .

What feelings have you experienced during this process?

. . . .

. . . .

. . . .

. . . .

. . . .

What do you want your relationship with God to be like?

. . . .

. . . .

. . . .

. . . .

. . . .

What steps are you prepared to take to grow in your relationship with God?

. . . .

. . . .

. . . .

. . . .

. . . .

WEEKEND Meditation from *Enjoy Today, Own Tomorrow* Declaration Cards

DO NOT BE ANXIOUS ABOUT ANYTHING, BUT IN EVERY SITUATION, BY PRAYER AND PETITION, WITH THANKSGIVING, PRESENT YOUR REQUESTS TO GOD.

Philippians 4:6

Take your time with journaling, meditation, and prayer before you move into week 7. Allow God to speak to you about your relationship with Him and His desires for you.

Week 7

REALIGNING YOUR LIFE

From My Heart to Yours

Dearest sister, we are so close to the end of our journey together. I am so overwhelmed on how courageous and bold you are! You have chosen to invest in yourself and to move forward victoriously. I am so grateful for you! Let's press on to realigning our lives with God so that we can live a balanced life centered in Him.

Let Us Pray

Dear Father, you have walked right beside us through this healing journey. Thank you that you have opened our eyes to the possibilities of being healed, being whole, and living a life we love. Lord, help us reprioritize our lives, so that we live more in your ways than in the ways of the world.

    Help us to design our daily lives where our relationships, habits, and lifestyle choices enable us to successfully live a life transformed walking in your power and love.

    In Jesus's name, amen!

Introduction

So far, you've considered the possibilities of realigning your life with God. You've looked at what your life could be as you reconnect to God and realign your life to His. The next step, then, moves in that direction. In this chapter, I begin to explain how to review your priorities and plan what your life will look like.

    In *Enjoy Today Own Tomorrow*, I wrote, "The most challenging part of this transition of creating new priorities and implementing new daily habits is focusing on the belief that this new lifestyle will bring success." Achieving success is important. Researcher Shawn

Achor found that people who become more optimistic, more socially connected, or just happier in their lives also become dramatically more successful. This week, focus on learning skills that can help you be more successful in your relationship with God and with others and in the way you live your life.

Day One

Picture what you want your realigned life to look like. What are your priorities? Your dreams? Your goals? Those are the first things to consider. If you don't know where you want to end up in this process, you'll never successfully get there. I shared about this process: "We must first establish our priorities and then lay out what our daily routine will look like. . . . In other words, we have to prioritize the areas of our lives that are meaningful and important to us."

Priorities determine everything else you do—the goals you set, how you spend your time, and how you relate to others. Without set priorities, your life can feel and even be out of control.

Three areas within your life need to be addressed: spiritual, relational, and health. I suggest that you use two questions to assess where you want your life to be: Where do you want to be in a year? Where do you want to be in five years? We'll look at each of those during days 1 through 3.

Reconnect with God: To assess where you want to be spiritually, adapt my questions to: Where do I want my relationship with God and my spiritual life to be in a year? Where do I want my relationship with God and my spiritual life to be in five years? Note that your spiritual assessment must take place with an eternal mindset. What you do in this life matters because of the promise of eternal life.

Begin with this very personal question: Do you believe that you will spend eternity in heaven when you die? As a believer, your response should be categorically *yes*! If you are not a believer in Jesus Christ, you are going to struggle with every other decision you make.

Realign your heart: I emphasized, "We must assess our lives and see whether we are living more in the world's ways than in God's ways. Do our lives line up with God's instructions, or do we live for selfish desires? This one decision is the beginning of how we design our days."

Compare these two lists and choose the word or phrase from each pair that best describes how you spend your time now:

WORLDLY DESIRES	SPIRITUAL DESIRES
ungodly	godly
controlled by personal desires	self-controlled by spiritual desires
impure and immoral	pure and moral
envious of what others have	affirming of what others have
using your gifts for profit or gain	using your gifts for God's glory

These actions and attitudes come from Titus 2:11–12 and Galatians 5:19–21. As you look at your responses to these, think about what you want your life to be like going forward. Describe your future life as you want it to be:

· ·

· ·

· ·

· ·

· ·

· ·

Reactivate your faith: Two scripture passages are listed above to help you look at how the worldly life differs from the spiritual life. There are many others. Read some or all of these verses or passages: Galatians 5:16; Colossians 3:5; 2 Timothy 2:4, 22; 1 Peter 2:5; 1 Peter 5:8; and 1 John 2:15–16. Which verse speaks to you most clearly? Use that verse as a prayer prompt and ask God to help you move closer to Him and the things that matter to Him.

"Priorities determine everything else you do—The goals you set, how you spend your time, and how you relate to others."

Day Two

After assessing where your relationship with God is, the next layer is to consider your relationships with others. If you are married, start with your spouse. If you are single or divorced, look at the person to whom you are the closest. Then, prioritize children, parents, friends, church community, and work associates.

Use my questions to guide your thinking: Where do you want your relationships to be in one year? In five years?

Reconnect with God: Draw a triangle and divide it by drawing horizontal lines slicing it into several sections. In the bottom section of the pyramid, write "God." In the next section above that, write your spouse's name or the person to whom you are closest. Move up to the next section and write the names of your children and parents. Continue providing names in sections of the people that are important to you. You'll hit a point where it is no longer possible to list every name and that's OK. Put a note there to remind you how that group of people relate to you.

With your pyramid complete, circle the names of the people who get most of your time. Do those you've circled also represent the people most important to you? If not, what do you need to change to create strong, balanced relationships based on your priorities and your relationship with God?

Realign your heart: Some relationships you've listed in your pyramid may be toxic. Toxic relationships are those that have behaviors that can emotionally and/or physically damage another. I described some of the signs of a person who is toxic: "narcissistic tendencies (always thinking of themselves before others), chronic judgmental conduct (excessively critical), unreliability, and untrustworthiness."

Look at your pyramid again and list any relationships that meet the criteria of being toxic below:

. . . .

. . . .

. . . .

. . . .

. . . .

. . . .

Christians often stay in toxic relationships too long because they desire to help and be supportive. But people who are toxic can damage you more than you can help them. My advice is to walk away immediately.

Reactivate your faith: You've identified the relationships that are most important to you and those that are damaging to you. Your pyramid shows you whether your life priorities reflect those important relationships in the way you spend your time. Your time is precious and limited.

Read 1 Corinthians 13:4–7. These beautiful words about love describe what relationships based on Christ should be like. Close this session by asking God to teach you how to love as these verses describe and to learn to balance your life so the way you spend your time reflects the priorities in your life.

"Create strong, balanced relationships based on your priorities and your relationship with God."

Day Three

$\mathcal{T}$he final area in your life is to assess your health. Overall, many Americans do not rank high on the state of their health. Our society values food that is fast and inexpensive, and we tend to reward ourselves with things that are not healthy. Additionally, America is high up on the list of countries that have the most cars per capita. That means we drive more and walk and bicycle less than many people in the world. All of that points to Americans' problem with obesity, lack of exercise, and poor health. On the other side, Americans have idolized those who are thin (often through unsafe diets) and who age well (often because of expensive treatments and surgeries).

Use today to consider your health carefully and honestly. Where do you want your health to be in a year? In five years? Decide that you want to take control of your health just as much as your relationships.

Reconnect with God: If you've seen a doctor recently, you probably have some idea of how your health is. Here's a small assessment to help you put your health in perspective:

Choose the option that most describes you:

Your diet:	is very healthy	is kind of healthy	is mostly junk food
Your energy:	is very high	comes and goes	is mostly nonexistent
Your body:	works for you	holds you back some	keeps you at home
Your exercise routine:	is sometimes too much	is well-balanced and safe	is nonexistent
Your sense of well-being	is very good	is OK but could be better	is terrible

I used my friend Kim Alexis's story to show how important it is to understand what your own body needs. It's important to look after your own well-being. Why? Read Genesis 1:27 and James 3:9. We are made in God's image, and our bodies have been created to bring Him glory. How we treat ourselves matters.

Realign your heart: Sometimes, the steps we take to regain our health and strengthen our sense of well-being need to be small and slow. Too often, we make a decision to make big changes in health and jump in wholeheartedly only to drop out because the demands are too great. Kim Alexis made several suggestions of small steps:

1. Simply move more by walking in your backyard or on your driveway.
2. Take a hot bath with Epsom salt to increase your heart rate.
3. Eat more healthy foods and snacks by making small changes at first.

Other small steps could include finding a walking buddy, spending more time outside, and keeping track of small changes in a journal. Other steps should include seeing your doctor regularly, getting yearly flu shots, having annual or biannual mammograms, and, beginning at the age of fifty, having colonoscopies every ten years.

Reactivate your faith: Why is assessing your health so important? Kim Alexis said, "I have a passion about prioritizing health because I know that ultimately, if we do good things for our bodies, then we can live as fully as God designed and to the best of our ability." God wants to use you, but your health could limit how. Make your health a priority that gets your priority time just as your relationship with God and with others does. It is that important.

Review the suggestions above and choose at least one to do this week. Commit that action to God and ask Him to guide you as you work to be the healthiest person you can be.

"We are made in God's image, and our bodies have been created to bring Him glory. How we treat ourselves matters."

Day Four

You've looked at three areas of priorities—your spiritual life, your relationships, and your health. With three days to assess those areas, you've probably identified areas that need attention as well as areas that are out of balance.

Today's discussion will address how we can develop habits that will allow us to keep our time and our priorities on what is most important in our lives. How do we do this? By desiring to pursue God as our highest priority, by putting our time and energy into the relationships that are most important to us, and by becoming as healthy as possible.

Reconnect with God: I point out that although most of us have tried in the past to put our lives in order, we may not have been able to bring about lasting change. Why is it that success does not come easily? Our success is based on how well we can develop good habits and disciplines in our lives—habits and disciplines that will last throughout our lives, not just for a short time.

I shared: "How do we choose good habits? By determining where we want to end up. What is it that you hope to achieve? Journal your goals. When you can answer the why behind what you are trying to achieve you can stay on point and be inspired to complete the task."

Before you get specific, answer these questions:

What changes have you made in the past that were unsuccessful? Why did they not succeed?

. . . .

. . . .

. . . .

. . . .

. . . .

. . . .

Why would this time be different if you tried to reclaim your life and live it based on the things that are most important to you?

. . . .

. . . .

. . . .

. . . .

. . . .

. . . .

Realign your heart: I researched the stories of successful people and came up with eight keys to their success. We'll look at four of those today and the other four tomorrow.

1. Get up early in the morning. This allowed them to put God first every day. Mark 1:35 documents that this was how Jesus began His day as well.
2. Read a lot. Spend time every day in God's Word. Scripture can fuel your soul just as food fuels your body. Jesus explained the importance of studying God's Word in John 6:51—through His word alone can we find eternal life.
3. Meditate with focused time thinking about and praying to God. Joshua 1:8 encouraged God's people to meditate on God's Word: "This Book of the Law shall not depart from your mouth, but you shall meditate in it day and night, that you may observe to do according to all that is written in it."
4. Prioritize health. See your body as God's temple and treat it accordingly. First Corinthians 6:19–20 instructs believers to remember that Christ bought their bodies through His sacrifice, so believers should use our bodies to glorify God.

Reactivate your faith: You've just looked at four ideas that could become daily habits in your life. These habits could be life-changing. Review the four ideas again. Which of these could bring balance to your life and move you toward how you want to live? Which of these are you willing to begin now?

After you've spent time thinking about the questions above, go to God in prayer. Ask Him for guidance as you work to realign your life to His. Sit in silence and let Him guide you to those habits that are most important to bring about the change you've acknowledged you want for your life.

"*Our success is based on how well we can develop good habits and disciplines in our lives.*"

Day Five

*Y*esterday, you looked at four habits of highly successful people. Each of these habits could teach you to be successful in realigning your life with God. Today, four more habits are presented. Evaluate them as carefully as you did the first four.

Reconnect with God: Below are the rest of the habits of highly successful people that I discovered:

1. Spend time with people who inspire you. Look for people who have achieved spiritual success in their lives and talk to them about what they've learned. Surround yourself with people whose lives reflect their alignment with God. First Thessalonians 5:11 encourages believers to edify each other, strengthening their faith along the journey.
2. Be goal-oriented. You've been encouraged along this process to record your goals and your dreams as well as your successes and your failures. Record your goals and then track how you're doing in meeting those.
3. Get enough sleep. Sleep is the answer to tiredness, anxiety, and worry. Sleep is also needed for the body to heal itself. Set a schedule for going to bed and rising in the morning and stick with it. Spend time in prayer at night, giving God your fears and concerns so that you can rest and sleep in Him.
4. Avoid wasting time. So many things around us can be time wasters. Social media and scrolling the internet steals hours of time that could have been used for more important things. I stated, "When we realize how temporal this world is and stay focused on the heavenly things then we can maximize our time daily."

Realign your heart: Look over the four suggestions given today. Just as you did yesterday, evaluate these four, using these questions: Which of these could bring balance to your life and move you toward how you want to live? Which of these are you willing to begin now?

You've now looked at eight suggestions that could become daily habits in your life and you've identified several as ideas to start immediately. One caution, however, is that trying to adapt all of these at one time is not a good idea. Start with one or at the most two at a time. Let them develop into a true habit before you begin to add more. Your goal is to bring about transformation in your life and realign your life with God's. That's a lifelong journey, so don't try to make it happen all at once.

Reactivate your faith: Commit the habits you've selected from the eight I provided to God. In your journal, write it or them (remember—one or two only) in your journal. Beside each, write the actions you'll take to create these habits in your life. For example, if you're going to get up earlier in the morning to spend time with God, record what time you'll set your alarm for. Recognize that you are committing this process to the Lord. What you are taking on is holy work. Don't take it lightly or try to do it too quickly. Rather, take this opportunity seriously. Take your time and do it right. And, make sure you give God the glory as He guides you in the process.

"That's a lifelong journey, so don't try to make it happen all at once."

Weekend Reflection

$\mathcal{T}$his week, you've assessed three areas of your life—your spiritual life, your relationships with others, and your health—and you've been encouraged to bring those into balance with your life priorities. You've also been encouraged to take action—to identify your priorities and to set goals for developing new habits in your life.

This weekend, begin to put those new habits into your daily schedule. Spend time with the Lord, asking for guidance as you step into new habits. Journal about how you feel taking on these new habits and priorities.

Over the weekend, journal about this week's experiences with these prompts:

What have you learned about you relationship with God right now?

....

....

....

....

....

....

What feelings have you experienced during this process?

....

....

....

....

....

What do you want your relationship with God to be like?

....

....

....

....

....

What steps are you prepared to take to grow in your relationship with God?

....

....

....

....

....

WEEKEND Meditation from *Enjoy Today, Own Tomorrow* Promise Cards

YOU WILL SHOW ME THE WAY OF LIFE,
    granting me the joy of your presence
    and the pleasures of living with you forever.

Psalm 16:11 NLT

Take your time with journaling, meditation, and prayer before you move into week 8. Allow God to speak to you about your relationship with Him and His desires for you.

Week 8

DISCOVERING AND REACTIVATING THE POWER WITHIN YOU

From My Heart to Yours

Dearest sister, I am so excited we have journeyed this far together. This week is so important because we stir up the power within us that is sure to bring healing. We realize that the power of God lives within us and when we call upon that power, then God works on our behalf! This is the life-giving power essential to overcoming and living a life we love. I hope you are as ready as I am to see yourself walking in the ultimate power of God every day!

Let Us Pray

Dear Father, thank you so very much that you did not leave us here on earth alone. Thank you that we literally have the living power of God residing within us. Thank you that you take our lives from ordinary to extraordinary when we live in your power. God, thank you that you gave us a helper, intercessor, and advocate for our lives called the Holy Spirit. Thank you, Lord, for your Holy Spirit power. It changes everything and makes a way for your plans to be fulfilled in our daily lives. Thank you that we are never alone and that you are always with us, living in and through us.

In Jesus's name, amen!

Introduction

This week, we'll be looking at a topic that doesn't often get a lot of study. That is the person of the Holy Spirit. We accept Him into our lives, but we don't always understand all that He does for us. We'll spend this entire week considering the six roles He takes on in our lives, the nine fruits that He brings into our lives, and the power He has.

I opened this chapter with the confession of not having had the ability on my own to forgive a business partner who had stolen from me. I wrote, "Truthfully, it's not entirely natural for any of us to be able to forgive, release our feelings about others, and move forward. It takes a supernatural event to truly walk out these very challenging acts. That is why the knowledge of, demonstration of, and activation of this inner power, called the Holy Spirit, is essential." As you focus on the Holy Spirit, ask God to help you see the Spirit with a deeper understanding of His work in your life.

Day One

I shared, "The Holy Spirit is actually the life-giving power that changes our ordinary into extraordinary. It is the power of the maker of the universe who created it all." The Holy Spirit works in our lives in six different ways or roles. We'll examine three of those roles today. And, the best way to understand the Holy Spirit is from Scripture. Jesus promised that the Holy Spirit would come into our lives: "And I will ask the Father, and he will give you another Advocate, who will never leave you. He is the Holy Spirit, who leads into all truth" (John 14:16 NLT).

Reconnect with God: The first two roles of the Holy Spirit are:

1. The Holy Spirit is your helper. The Holy Spirit is there when you are in despair as your greatest helper. He supports you, comforts you, and guides you during difficult times. Read more about how the Holy Spirit is your help in John 14:26. Based on what you've read, how have you experienced His help?

. . . .

. . . .

. . . .

. . . .

. . . .

2. The Holy Spirit is your advocate. As your advocate, the Holy Spirit goes before God to plead for you. He defends and protects you. He helps you fight your battles and lets you know that you are not alone. Read John 14:16 again. Based on what you've read, how have you experienced His advocating for you?

. . . .

. . . .

. . . .

. . . .

. . . .

. . . .

Realign your heart: The third role of the Holy Spirit is found in how your heart realigns to God's:

3. The Holy Spirit is your intercessor. Whether you have the words or not, the Holy Spirit intercedes for you in prayer. He will speak for you when you don't have the words. He communicates with God on your behalf. Read more about how the Holy Spirit is your intercessor in Romans 8:26–27. Based on what you've read, how have you experienced His intercession between God and you?

. . . .

. . . .

. . . .

. . . .

. . . .

Reactivate your faith: I emphasized the gift of the Holy Spirit with these words: "God loves us so much He gave up His only Son to die on the Cross, resurrected Him into heaven, and gave us the Holy Spirit so that a part of Jesus would live on through each one of us." The gift of the Holy Spirit in your life is precious. Read over the first three roles of the Holy Spirit in your life again. Then, go to God in prayer. Acknowledge His grace and mercy in your life. Acknowledge His sacrificial gift of His Son on your behalf. Acknowledge His gift of the Holy Spirit in your life and ask Him to lead you to grow into your knowledge and understanding of how the Holy Spirit works in you.

"The Holy Spirit is actually the life-giving power that changes our ordinary into extraordinary."

Day Two

As we continue to study the roles of the Holy Spirit, let's go back to the passage in John in which Jesus promised the Holy Spirit to us. John 14:17 continues Jesus's explanation of the Holy Spirit: "The world cannot receive him, because it isn't looking for him and doesn't recognize him. But you know him, because he lives with you now and later will be in you" (NLT).

The Holy Spirit has been given to us specifically to be with us and to dwell with us. Yesterday, we looked at how the Holy Spirit is our helper, our advocate, and our intercessor. Today, we look at three more roles that He fills in our lives.

Reconnect with God: Two more roles of the Holy Spirit are:

1. The Holy Spirit is our counselor. This means we have direct input from God in our lives—His counsel, His assistance, His advice, His wisdom, and His support. We can depend upon the Holy Spirit to guide us in His ways, not ours. Read more about how the Holy Spirit is your counselor in Romans 11:34, 36. Based on what you've read, how have you experienced His counsel and assistance between God and you?

2. The Holy Spirit is the Spirit of truth. The Holy Spirit reveals God's truth to us and God's plan and desires for us. Read more about how the Holy Spirit reveals God's truth in John 16:13. Based on what you've read, how have you experienced God's revelation of truth through the Holy Spirit?

. . . .

. . . .

. . . .

. . . .

. . . .

Realign your heart: The final role of the Holy Spirit shows just how great God's gift of the Holy Spirit is in our lives.

3. The Holy Spirit is God Himself in us. The Almighty God has all authority and power. There will never be anyone or anything that is more powerful. Read 1 Corinthians 2:10 about how God the Spirit lives with you. Based on what you've read, how have you experienced God's indwelling of the Holy Spirit within you?

. . . .

. . . .

. . . .

. . . .

. . . .

Reactivate your faith: I wrote, "There is no other authority or power greater than God. We are humans in great need of a Savior. We will never live purely enough to have full access to God in the natural. It is only through the Holy Spirit that we can move into God's presence. When we give God our lives and declare His Son Jesus as the Lord and Savior of our lives, then a piece of Him takes residence with us."

Read my statement above slowly—at least twice more. Note that God gave us the Holy Spirit because we will never be perfect enough to come into God's presence on our own. God alone could arrange that for us.

Close this session by meditating on this gift that allows you direct connection to God, even though you will never be good enough to deserve it on your own.

"The Holy Spirit has been given to us specifically to be with us and to dwell with us."

Day Three

*T*hrough the work of the Holy Spirit in our lives, we are able to produce fruit—fruit that comes through Him. That means that our lives begin to take on the very characteristics of God. You may have already memorized these fruits of the Spirit as a child in Sunday school. Paul named them in Galatians 5:22–23: "But the fruit of the Spirit is love, joy, peace, forbearance, kindness, goodness, faithfulness, gentleness and self-control."

All of these are spiritual characteristics that we could not develop on our own. Yet, through the Holy Spirit, these become evident in our lives as we grow and mature in our relationship with the Father. We'll look at most of these tomorrow. Today, we'll focus only on the fruit of love.

Reconnect with God: Love is the most important fruit of the Spirit because it reflects the very core of who God is. God *is* love. Jesus is the visual manifestation of God's love. First John 4:8 states, "Whoever does not love does not know God, because God is love."

Through Him, we can see what true sacrificial love—the kind of love that led Jesus to the Cross—looks like. In Greek, there are four words for love and each have totally different meanings. British theologian and author C. S. Lewis in his book *The Four Loves* defined them this way:

Storge is empathy love and is expressed fondness through and familiarity with family members and others.

Philia (or *phileo*) is the love between friends. It is love based on a strong connection with shared values and interests.

Eros is romantic love. This refers more to being in love with someone than erotic love.

Agape is the unconditional love of God. Agape love exists regardless of how circumstances change and is selfless.

God loves us with *agape* love. Jesus died for us through *agape* love. And the Holy Spirit dwells within us to teach us how to love as they love us.

Realign your heart: *Agape* love is both a feeling and an action. It cannot be only a feeling. Because *agape* love comes from God, we demonstrate that love in the way we act and in the things we do. *Agape* love demands response. Think of it this way: What difference would Jesus's love for us have made if He hadn't willingly taken on our sin as His own? His love was an action and His love requires action from us as well. Read 1 Corinthians 13:4-8 to see how *agape* love is described in scripture.

How has the Holy Spirit taught you *agape* love? How do you show that love to others?

. . . .

. . . .

. . . .

. . . .

. . . .

. . . .

Reactivate your faith: In Matthew 22:36–39, Jesus was asked which was the most important commandment. Jesus responded that the greatest commandment is to love God completely—with our hearts, our souls, and our minds. Second, however, was the commandment to love others the same way we love ourselves.

How does Jesus's response demonstrate *agape* love? How difficult is it to live out these instructions?

. . . .

. . . .

. . . .

. . . .

. . . .

. . . .

If you're completely honest with yourself, you've probably realized that we can't fulfill Jesus's directions on our own. What is required is supernatural love—love that is different than any other love we've experienced. That supernatural love—*agape* love—can only grow in us out of the power of the Holy Spirit. It is impossible for us to achieve that kind of love on our own.

Close in prayer, asking God to help you grow in your ability to supernaturally love others as He loves you.

"Through the work of the Holy Spirit in our lives, we are able to produce fruit—fruit that comes through Him."

Day Four

*T*oday's discussion will include the other eight fruits of the Spirit. Each of these also reflect the character of God. Like we saw with the fruit of love, these are supernatural qualities that can only be found in our lives through the presence of the Holy Spirit. Each of these characteristics are words we use a lot. However, our understanding of each word and characteristic is not the supernatural characteristic that comes from God.

Reconnect with God: As you study these eight fruits of the Spirit, seek to see how God's supernatural characteristic differs from how you understand these words. Be prepared to redefine each of these as you go.

1. *Joy* is more than being happy. We use the term *joyful* to describe what it feels like to have joy. However, this fruit of the Spirit is supernatural joy. It comes out of the battle of life when we concentrate on God instead of our struggles. (Read John 16:22 and Hebrews 12:2 for examples of spiritual joy.)
2. *Peace* can be understood as a state of tranquility or quiet. We tend to grasp for peace when we're fighting with others or when the chaos of life overwhelms us. But God's supernatural peace is a calmness—a resting, if you will—that can only be found when we lean into and depend upon God. (Read Isaiah 55:12 for a picture of supernatural peace.)
3. *Forbearance* can also be defined as patience and tolerance. It's more than just tolerating something that's annoying. Rather, supernatural forbearance leads to unity and harmony. It's demonstrated through displaying grace to others. (Read Galatians 6:9 for a picture of supernatural forbearance.)

Before moving on, evaluate how these three fruits of the Spirit can be seen in your life. Typically, these are things we desire in our lives. We look for happiness in our work and our relationships. We design our homes to be peaceful and pleasant. We strive to be patient, even when sitting in traffic or at a doctor's office, and we talk about being tolerant. Yet, none of these efforts on our part will ever satisfy these spiritual hungers. Are you struggling to find these? Or, are you discovering how these can be developed only through the work of the Holy Spirit? Where are you on this journey?

Realign your heart: The next three characteristics are again words we use every day and they are characteristics we try to teach our children. Again, however, our cultural understanding of these words does not reflect God's character.

4. *Kindness* in general is becoming rare in our society. People are in such a hurry that they don't often take time to be kind to one another. Supernatural kindness is more than just being nice to someone. Supernatural kindness includes giving mercy as we are kind, even when the person to whom it is given is unworthy. I described kindness as "the currency of heaven." (Read Ephesians 2:6–7 for a picture of supernatural kindness.)

5. *Goodness* has become an old-fashioned, somewhat archaic word in our society. People don't tend to strive for goodness—being decent to others and being honorable in everything we do. Yet, it is what God expects of us. In Psalm 23, David described God's goodness and mercy as eternal. God is the same yesterday, today, and tomorrow. He embodies supernatural goodness and mercy and expects us to show those characteristics to others. Why? Because it's how we reveal to the world who God is and that we are His. (Read Matthew 5:16 and Acts 10:38 for a picture of supernatural goodness.)

6. *Faithfulness* means that we are true to our word. We follow through with what we promise to do. Relationships thrive when people can trust each other and suffer when they cannot. Because God is faithful, we are also called to a supernatural level of faithfulness and trustworthiness. (Read Hebrews 11:1 and Proverbs 19:21 for a picture of supernatural faithfulness.)

Again, take time to evaluate how these three fruits of the Spirit can be seen in your life. Are you struggling with these? Why?

Reactivate your faith: The final two fruits of the Spirit are gentleness and self-control:

7. *Gentleness* that is supernatural usually is developed intentionally through the Holy Spirit. Gentleness requires controlling anger and hotheadedness and is seen in mildness of behavior. In *Enjoy Today Own Tomorrow*, I encouraged, "Lean into your inner Holy Spirit power and remind yourself that God needs all of us to stand up in gentleness and show the world its beauty." (Read Matthew 6:14–15 for an example of supernatural gentleness.)

8. *Self-control* is a fruit of the Spirit, and it is also required in each of the other fruits of the Spirit. Even with the Holy Spirit's guidance, we still have to decide intentionally to listen to His counsel and to follow His guidance. To do that requires intentionally deciding not to do otherwise—not to be mean to someone who clearly deserves it, not to speak harshly to someone who has been rude, not to wallow in self-pity but seek His joy instead. (Read Matthew 26:53–54 for an amazing picture of supernatural self-control.)

I concluded, "The Holy Spirit empowers us to move through the supernatural powers of God. We suddenly gain abilities to do things we could never do on our own." Don't underestimate your part in this process. The Holy Spirit dwells within you, and He's constantly ready to assist you. But you have to be willing to listen, intentional in your response to His guidance and ready to allow Him to bring about change in your life. Are you ready for that kind of transformation? Talk it over with God and let Him show you areas in your life that don't reflect these supernatural fruits of the Spirit.

"The Holy Spirit empowers us to move through the supernatural powers of God. We suddenly gain abilities to do things we could never do on our own."

We'll conclude this week by considering the Holy Spirit's power. I wrote, "The power of the Holy Spirit is the same power that created our entire universe." Read Genesis 1:1–2 and focus on how God took nothing and yet created everything. I emphasized, "We have the ability to create whatever we pursue with this inner power that gives us the creative energy to build something out of nothing as well."

Reconnect with God: I share three ways the Holy Spirit's power interacts with our world.

First, the Holy Spirit has the ability to bring dead things to life—He has resurrection power. I share the example of how the Holy Spirit resurrected my dead marriage to one that is healthy and joyful.

Have you seen the Holy Spirit's resurrection power in your life? Maybe He resurrected a relationship that had become so broken that you didn't think it could be healed. Maybe He resurrected a career that you thought you would never be able to do again.

Think through your life. How have you seen the Holy Spirit bring something back to life that you thought was dead?

. . . .

. . . .

. . . .

. . . .

. . . .

How does it make you feel to know that God's resurrection power was extended to you through His Spirit?

....
....
....
....
....
....

Realign your heart: Second, the Holy Spirit can change things and influence the environment, sometimes through us. His power can produce holy visions and dreams, make miracles happen, set up divine appointments, and open doors to help us fulfill His plans.

Below, record examples of how you've seen the Holy Spirit use this power:

Through holy visions and dreams:

....
....
....
....
....
....

Through miracles:

. . . .

. . . .

. . . .

. . . .

. . . .

Through divine appointments:

. . . .

. . . .

. . . .

. . . .

. . . .

Through opening doors:

. . . .

. . . .

. . . .

. . . .

. . . .

As you reflect on these actions, you may realize that the Holy Spirit has been involved in your life in ways you hadn't realized.

Reactivate your faith: Third, the Holy Spirit is our source of hope. I defined hope as "a desire with expectation of obtainment or fulfillment or an expectation embodied with confidence and trust." Hope isn't a wish, like hoping we'll get what we want at Christmas. Rather, hope is the expectation of what God is going to do in our lives and through us.

Read Romans 15:13. Conclude in prayer, asking the Holy Spirit to teach you to hold onto your hope in what God is doing and will do in your life.

"We have the ability to create whatever we pursue with this inner power that gives us the creative energy to build something out of nothing as well."

Weekend Reflection

This week, you've spent time learning about the work of the Holy Spirit in your life. I stated, "The Holy Spirit is the only way God is revealed to us and moves through us." This weekend, spend time reviewing the roles of the Holy Spirit, the fruit of the Spirit, and the power of the Holy Spirit. Consider memorizing 1 John 4:4: "You are of God, little children, and have overcome them, because He who is in you is greater than he who is in the world."

Over the weekend, journal about this week's experiences with these prompts:

What have your learned about your relationship with God right now?

. . . .

. . . .

. . . .

. . . .

. . . .

. . . .

What feelings have you experienced during this process?

....

....

....

....

....

What do you want your relationship with God to be like?

....

....

....

....

....

What steps are you prepared to take to grow in your relationship with God?

....

....

....

....

....

WEEKEND Meditation from *Enjoy Today, Own Tomorrow* Declaration Cards

I PRAY THAT OUT OF HIS GLORIOUS RICHES HE MAY STRENGTHEN YOU WITH POWER THROUGH his Spirit in your inner being, so that Christ may dwell in your hearts through faith. And I pray that you, being rooted and established in love, may have power, together with all the Lord's holy people, to grasp how wide and long and high and deep is the love of Christ.

Ephesians 3:16–18

Take your time with journaling, meditation, and prayer before you move into week 9. Allow God to speak to you about your relationship with Him and His desires for you.

Week 9

REACTIVATE BY PAYING IT FORWARD

From My Heart to Yours

Dearest sister, we are nearing the finish line with just a few more steps left. We have started the healing process together. I know it is a long and sometimes not so fun journey, but now we have more tools and applications to find complete healing. From this point forward, God is counting on us to share this hope with others! We must share with the world that He is in fact still moving and healing right now, today!

I urge you to pay this forward to others who are hurting and wounded. We become the hands and feet for God to reach others who are in great pain. We have the tools and knowledge now to help others find healing, just like you did. We are the hope the world needs today.

God was so generous that He gave us His only Son, Jesus, and allowed Him to be crucified on a Cross for us, even as wretched sinners. We, too, must be generous with our testimony, time, talents, and treasures.

Let Us Pray

Dear Generous Father, thank you that you loved us so much that you gave your only Son to die for us. Lord, help us to use all the gifts and healing that you have given us for your glory. Lord, use our healing story to bring glory to your name. Lord, please help me be your hands and feet and to love the hurting so that they, too, may be healed.

In Jesus's name, amen.

Introduction

To this point, we've worked through the process of complete healing. That doesn't necessarily mean that you have achieved complete healing. It's a process—a journey—that takes time. But, as you've confronted the pain in your life, you've also acknowledged the work that God continues to do. At this point, have you wondered, *How can I pay it forward? How could God use me?*

The answer is simple: "We are God's mouthpieces. We are His hands and feet. He is counting on us to be vessels of His goodness and generosity. We can be the start of an answer to the hurting and the lost. We can be the conduits to the world for bringing relief to the needy. We can and should pay generous acts forward to enjoy today and own our tomorrow" (*Enjoy Today Own Tomorrow*). With that in mind, this chapter is about developing generosity in order to pay it forward.

Day One

Finedictionary.com gives several definitions for *generosity*. One is "the quality of being noble; noble-mindedness." Isn't it interesting that the first definition is not about giving, but about who the giver is on the inside. Being *noble-minded* is defined as being "of high moral or intellectual value." *Noble-minded* is not a phrase we use often, but it reflects a life that is dedicated to things of God. Paul encouraged the Philippians to search for the things that are of God: "Finally, brothers and sisters, whatever is true, whatever is noble, whatever is right, whatever is pure, whatever is lovely, whatever is admirable—if anything is excellent or praiseworthy—think about such things" (4:8).

Another definition the Fine Dictionary gives is, "liberality in giving; munificence." An interesting point to note in the definition of *generosity* is the definition of *munificence*, which the Fine Dictionary explains as "a giving or bestowing with extraordinary liberality; generous bounty; lavish generosity."

When we think about our generosity that comes in response to God's generosity given to us, both of these definitions are important and can guide us as we consider how we pay it forward.

Reconnect with God: Researchers have found that there are great benefits in developing a life of generosity. One study gave participants $100. Half were asked to spend the money on themselves; half were asked to spend the money on others. Those who spent the money on others reported higher levels of happiness than the other group. Another study found that being generous can actually boost our moods.

Think through that research carefully. Why do you think responding in generosity to what God has done for us would have mental and emotional benefits for us?

· ·

· ·

· ·

· ·

· ·

· ·

Realign your heart: Another benefit of generosity is physical. Researchers have found that those with a lifestyle of generosity often live longer lives. Generous individuals often experience lower blood pressure, the same that can be achieved through medications or exercise. And there's support socially from others. On the other hand, researchers found that people who have a lifestyle of stinginess face internal shame and higher levels of the stress hormone cortisol.

Review the definitions of *noble-mindedness* and *generosity* above. Why do you think our generosity or our stinginess can impact our health so deeply?

· ·

· ·

· ·

· ·

· ·

· ·

Possibly the answer to research findings are explained in Titus 3:8: "This is a trustworthy saying. And I want you to stress these things, so that those who have trusted in God may be careful to devote themselves to doing what is good. These things are excellent and profitable for everyone." Because of our relationship with God, our response should be devoting ourselves to doing what is good in the sight of God. God has shown us extraordinarily lavish generosity. Are we to do less?

Reactivate your faith: Generosity of spirit. Generosity of sharing. Generosity in life. God wants us to model what we have received to others. Jesus called His disciples to what is good and right before God: "A good man brings good things out of the good stored up in his heart, and an evil man brings evil things out of the evil stored up in his heart. For the mouth speaks what the heart is full of" (Luke 6:45).

Paul also explained this idea of being noble-minded and generous. Read Romans 2:1–2, 9–13, and Romans 15:5–6. Journal about what being noble-minded (having the mind of God) looks like in your life. Then, offer yourself to God for Him to teach you to truly have the mind of God in all things, especially in your response to His generosity to you.

> *"When we think about our generosity that comes in response to God's generosity given to us, both of these definitions are important and can guide us as we consider how we pay it forward."*

Day Two

*O*ur generosity includes more than what we give to others: "We can begin with being a mouthpiece of truth—because we all have a story to share. No one gets through this life with distressing experiences" (*Enjoy Today Own Tomorrow*).

Our experiences become the point where we can give generously to another. I asked, "When we see someone facing the same hurt we have been through, what should we do?" (117). Today, seek an answer to that question.

Reconnect with God: I outlined two ways we can be generous in how we respond to people in faith. First, I pointed out that "one of the greatest gifts we can give to God is being a witness for Him." I proposed that we can make a difference in the lives of those who are hurting in ways that we have hurt by sharing our own stories. "Telling others about what God has done for us is the best way to live out a purpose-filled life. God expects us to share the good news of His healing power."

Think about times when you've experienced God's power in your life. Possibilities could include through the death of a loved one or a marriage, the loss of a relationship, or walking through a horrible medical diagnosis. These are just a few examples to get you thinking. List your experiences below:

. . . .

. . . .

. . . .

. . . .

. . . .

How have you used these experiences to share your witness of what God has done in your life?

. . . .

. . . .

. . . .

. . . .

. . . .

If you haven't used them as a witness, explain why you haven't.

. . . .

. . . .

. . . .

. . . .

Often, we're so embarrassed or stressed by what we're experiencing that we try to hide the pain from others. However, it is through that pain that our witness of what God has done becomes the stronger and more real. It is that witness that can change the lives of others.

Realign your heart: I explained that "paying our story forward is an effective weapon against the devil. . . . We defeat the enemy with the name of Jesus and the word of our testimonies about what God has done in our lives. When we share our story of victory, it totally disarms the enemy."

How do you think your story of faith can defeat Satan?

....

....

....

....

....

....

Your story has power! I emphasized: "If we share our victorious testimonies through the blood of Jesus, then the enemy must flee. The devil is defeated, and the captive is set free. This is exactly how God needs us to operate."

Reactivate your faith: The second way we can pay it forward with generosity is with our finances. Everything we have comes from God and belongs to Him. Everything. Colossians 1:16 states, "For in him all things were created: things in heaven and on earth, visible and invisible, whether thrones or powers or rulers or authorities; all things have been created through him and for him." And, 1 Corinthians 10:26 states, "The earth is the Lord's, and everything in it."

Memorize 1 Corinthians 10:26 then meditate on that verse. How does your life reflect His ownership? Are you free with your story of faith? With your witness? With your possessions?

. . . .

. . . .

. . . .

. . . .

. . . .

. . . .

Spend time in prayer as you contemplate the answers to those questions. Ask God to teach you how He wants you to respond to His generosity.

"Our experiences become the point where we can give generously to another."

Day Three

*T*he story of Cain and Abel is one of jealousy and greed. Genesis 4:2–8 records the story. While many lessons can be drawn from the passage, one seems to stand out above the others. When the brothers made offerings to God, Abel's was accepted and Cain's was not. Why? Abel's offering was described as the firstfruits—the best of what he had to give. Cain's was described as "some of the fruits"—not the best, but possibly the leftovers. One offering honored God; the other disappointed Him.

Today, keep this truth in mind: "If we give God our first fruits and our best, then He will always take care of us in every way" (*Enjoy Today Own Tomorrow*). Proverbs 3:9–10 states:

Honor the Lord with your wealth,
   with the firstfruits of all your crops;
then your barns will be filled to overflowing,
   and your vats will brim over with new wine.

What we do with our offerings should bring honor to God.

Reconnect with God: I pointed out that "God doesn't need our money. He wants to see if we trust Him. God asks that we tithe (that's a 10 percent offering of our income) to the church we attend each week. . . . God requires very little when it comes to money."

Offerings are gifts given above the tithe. How can these offerings—things that go beyond what is required—show a generous spirit and a deeper level of trust in Him?

....

....

....

....

....

....

Read Luke 6:38. How does God reward your generosity that grows from your faith in Him?

....

....

....

....

....

Realign your heart: There are other ways to be generous than just with our financial offerings. I suggested two overall areas in which we can give generously:

First, we can be generous in prayer: Spend "a dedicated portion of our week supporting others" in prayer. Create a prayer list to use today by reflecting on the needs you know within these areas:

- Loved ones, friends, and acquaintances
- Churches, pastors, and other church leaders
- The president, governmental leaders, and other world leaders
- Specific ministries and missions and for finances to support their work
- Safety and protection

Commit to using this list for the rest of the week, updating it as you receive information. "Praying for others intimately is a great way to be generous."

Second, we can be generous with our talents. Determine what you do well. Use the list below to jump-start your evaluation of what your talents are that God can use. Circle each thing you can do.

- Painting, building, indoor repairs, yardwork, cleaning homes, sewing
- Singing, playing an instrument, designing costumes and sets, creativity
- Travel, missions work, care
- Cooking, hospitality
- Bible study, teaching, leadership, organization, administration

Review those you've circled. How are you generously using these talents for God now?

. . . .

. . . .

. . . .

. . . .

. . . .

. . . .

How could you be more generous with how God has gifted you? Think specifically of opportunities that you know are available. Also, consider how you could use your talents by creating new opportunity.

. . . .

. . . .

. . . .

. . . .

. . . .

. . . .

Reactivate your faith: Our generosity is part of our response to God. It is a holy response and is meant to bring glory to God, not to ourselves. Matthew 6:1 states, "Be careful not to practice your righteousness in front of others to be seen by them. If you do, you will have no reward from your Father in heaven."

Keep that verse in mind as you pray through the list of prayer concerns you made earlier. Also, pray through the talents you've been given and ask God to show you where your efforts can bring glory to Him.

"If we give God our first fruits and our best, then He will always take care of us in every way."

Day Four

I presented this quotation from 2 Corinthians 9:6–7 (CEV):

A FEW SEEDS MAKE
  a small harvest,
but a lot of seeds make
  a big harvest.

Each of you must make up your own mind about how much to give. But don't feel sorry that you must give and don't feel that you are forced to give.

How do you determine how to approach generosity in your life?

Reconnect with God: Your giving and your generosity connect you to God. Here's how:

1. Generous giving shows your trust in and dependence upon God.
2. God loves a cheerful giver (2 Corinthians 9:7*b*).
3. God has already blessed you abundantly and will continue to do so.
4. Giving is an "overflowing in many expressions of thanks to God" (2 Corinthians 9:12).

Meditate on those statements. Then read 2 Corinthians 9:6–15. Respond to these questions:

Do you see your giving to God as a joy or a requirement? Why?

. . . .

. . . .

. . . .

. . . .

. . . .

Where do you see generosity in what you do for and give for God?

. . . .

. . . .

. . . .

. . . .

How do you see God blessing your generosity?

. . . .

. . . .

. . . .

. . . .

Realign your heart: I wrote, "God matches our giving. If we give a little, our harvest is little. But if we give big, then our harvest is plentiful. He leaves it up to our hearts. God never forces us to give. But He loves a cheerful heart and the people who give. God will supply all we need."

The word *joyful* can be understood as:

Delightful	Gleeful
Elated	Jubilant
Full of joy	Very glad

The word *sorrowful* can be understood as:

Dejected	Full of sorrow
Distressed	Sad

Which of these words best describe how you feel when giving?

. . . .

. . . .

. . . .

. . . .

. . . .

. . . .

Would you like your feelings about giving to change? Why?

. . . .

. . . .

. . . .

. . . .

. . . .

. . . .

Reactivate your faith: I wrote, "He also promises we will always have something to give to others. He will increase what we have so we can give generously. Most importantly, the greatest reward is that others will see the generous face of God through our actions."

This session has given you the opportunity to evaluate your giving and your generosity. You may not be happy with where you are right this moment, but that can change. Give your giving over to the Lord. Ask Him to teach you how to trust Him in a way that allows you to step out in faith with your giving. Ask God to teach you generosity of spirit and then show you how to approach your life in the spirit of generosity.

"He leaves giving up to our hearts. God never forces us to give. But He loves a cheerful heart and the people who give. God will supply all we need."

Day Five

*I*n a society that judges wealth based on who has the most, the concept of giving generously for the glory of God is completely countercultural. Jesus's statement that we are more blessed by giving than receiving is as hard for our society to accept as it was for His original hearers.

As we conclude this week of examining how our stories can pay forward to others, keep in mind that what Jesus taught is that God expects us to be different than the world around us. He expects us to go against the culture rather than support it.

Reconnect with God: I presented Jordan and Nicki Rubin as an example of taking Jesus's countercultural teachings to heart. I wrote that "they believe that paying it forward is essential to living out the life Christ died for us to live." They based their understanding of paying it forward on two scripture verses—Matthew 10:42 and Luke 12:48. Read these two verses and then note below the truths in these verses.

How do these truths encourage paying it forward?

. . . .

. . . .

. . . .

. . . .

. . . .

. . . .

Realign your heart: Jordan and Nicki explain how paying it forward aligns their hearts to God's: "Paying it forward shows [others] the love of God. It basically shows somebody that God loves them so much He can cause anyone, anywhere, to answer a prayer. Whether it is a financial need, an encouragement, or both, it's something we love to do. We give because we know we're truly giving to God. We are also trying to treat somebody the way we would like to be treated."

Focus on this statement: "God loves them so much He can cause anyone, anywhere, to answer a prayer."

How has God caused you to do something for someone that you later found out was an answer to a prayer? How did you find out it was an answer to a prayer?

. . . .

. . . .

. . . .

. . . .

. . . .

Reactivate your faith: Paying it forward leaves an indelible footprint of how we interact with the world. I encourage you to imagine how many people we could impact if we showed generosity of giving of ourselves. I wrote, "Living beyond ourselves and in the power of the Holy Spirit, giving as God would give, and helping the needy reassures our focus is heavenward and on the eternal versus the natural."

Conclude this session by considering what you do and who you could become in Him if you used all you've been given to pay it forward. Ask God to show you the possibilities for your life.

"God expects us to be different than the world around us."

Weekend Reflection

This week, you've spent time evaluating how to pay it forward through generosity. This weekend, continue to think about areas of generosity in your life. Challenge yourself to look for opportunities in which God can use you to care for others and bring glory to Him.

Take time to relax and rest and to listen and pray. Allow yourself time to be still in Him. Then, over the weekend, journal about this week's experiences with these prompts:

What have your learned about your relationship with God right now?

· ·

· ·

· ·

· ·

· ·

· ·

What feelings have you experienced during this process?

· ·

· ·

· ·

· ·

· ·

What do you want your relationship with God to be like?

· ·

· ·

· ·

· ·

· ·

What steps are you prepared to take to grow in your relationship with God?

· ·

· ·

· ·

· ·

· ·

WEEKEND Meditation from *Enjoy Today, Own Tomorrow* Declaration Cards

THEY TRIUMPHED OVER HIM
  by the blood of the Lamb
  and by the word of their testimony.

Revelation 12:11

Take your time with journaling, meditation, and prayer before you move into week 10. Allow God to speak to you about your relationship with Him and His desires for you.

MY RECONNECT, REALIGN, REACTIVATE STORY

From My Heart to Yours

Dearest sister, this week I am so proud of you because I know you have had to really dig deep and press in to experience amazing triumphs over your trials. It brings me such honor and humility to guide you through a life-transforming journey walking out of your hurts into healing. I thank God for making a message out of my mess and allowing me to share my story of how He healed me through every test, trial, tragedy, and trauma as God wrote a healing story in my heart creating a testimony that He is still healing the hurt today!

Let Us Pray

Dear Lord, I pray, thank you today that you have rescued, delivered, and healed us through your unconditional love and relentless pursuit of us. Lord, no matter what we faced, you, O God, were with us every step of the way and loved us through it all.

Thank you for writing our story through your amazing grace that helped us walk out of our hurts into healing.

Lord, we know that we now can share this truth that YOU are still healing and moving today through our lives supernaturally. We know that every time we share our testimony of how you have healed our broken hearts that others will experience healing too!

Father, thank you for loving us, and, together, we will help others discover the power to live the life they love and defeat the enemy over and over!

In Jesus's name, the name above all names, we pray. Amen.

Introduction

Our study of chapter 10 will be different than anything we've done up to now. The reason for that is because chapter 10 itself is different than all the other chapters. Chapter 10 is personal. It's intimate. It's transparent. And it's very real.

In chapter 10, I put my story together. I shared my struggles and my pains. I revealed the hurt and despair I worked through. I outlined my tough road back to reconnecting my life with God, realigning my heart with His, and reactivating my faith. This book could not have been written without that journey.

Why was I willing to lay my soul bare? I said, "I poured my heart out by sharing my story to equip you with the tools to discover the power within. My passion explodes when I see that you have found hope, power, and are truly living the life you love!"

I have put it all in print for you. And you've now worked through the pieces of the journey to find healing through God. This week, as you hear about the steps I took from my personal story, you'll have a chance to put your story down as well.

Day One

My story began in struggle. I described myself as being "blind and could not see, . . . deaf and could not hear, . . . lame and could not walk, [and] . . . mute and could not speak." I felt empty, hopeless, and lifeless, and I was looking for a miracle.

Begin your story with a description of what your life was like when you were disconnected from God. Were you flailing wildly trying to find something to grab onto? Begin your story.

. . . .

. . . .

. . . .

. . . .

. . . .

. . . .

Reconnect with God: I realized that what I really needed was to have an encounter with God unlike anything I had experienced before. But I struggled with my understanding of God. I questioned why He had allowed me to get so far away from Him. I wondered who He really was. In that time of questions about who He was, I dared myself to surrender my life to Him. I wrote that I surrendered my entire life—my "sins, shame, past, dreams, children, marriage, heart, and religious beliefs."

Now it's your turn. What questions toward God did you struggle with in despair? What were you willing to do to turn back to Him? Tell your story.

. . . .

. . . .

. . . .

. . . .

. . . .

. . . .

Realign your heart: Another thing I struggled with was opening myself up to the power of the Holy Spirit. I was fearful of people who believed things I didn't understand, like the gift of tongues or the miraculous power of God. My fear caused me to push away from anything that could be of God that I didn't understand. My fear grew out of my understanding of God at that point in time and reflected my past religious training. My fear could have become the limiting factor of what I was willing to do for healing.

What questions have you struggled with about where God was in your pain? How did you find answers to them? Have your past religious experiences helped you come back to God, or did they create barriers that made it difficult to move toward Him? Tell your story.

. . . .

. . . .

. . . .

. . . .

. . . .

Reactivate your faith: I described how I fell on my knees before God and cried out to Him in complete surrender. I then challenged God to come to my rescue if He loved me. I waited, expecting Him to "pour Himself into me and reconnect my soul and spirit back into His love and power. That day, I felt my heart lifted enough so I could breathe. . . . A supernatural feeling of peace and comfort started flowing through me like never before. It was as though my heart knew that no matter what I was facing, God loved me intimately" (131).

Describe how you came back to God. Were you emotional? Did you have expectations of how God would respond? Tell your story:

. . . .

. . . .

. . . .

. . . .

. . . .

. . . .

Close this time of telling your story by thanking God for what He has done and what He continues to do in your life.

"What I really needed was to have an encounter with God unlike anything I had experienced before."

Day Two

As I reached out in pain and desperation, I discovered who God was for the first time. That was the point that my life changed as God began to change me.

As you read more of my journey, let my words help you recall the specifics of your own journey.

Reconnect with God: I shared my first experience with reconnecting to God. I explained that He restored within me all those things I didn't have: "the blind eyes of my heart were opened. I saw God for who He really is for the first time. I recognized a God who loves us all so extravagantly right where we are–even in our greatest weaknesses. My ears heard a new sound–God's voice in my heart for the first time. My lame soul and spirit came alive again. I now had hope where there had been none. My tongue loudly declared the restoring love and goodness of God to everyone who would listen!"

Describe what you experienced when you came back to God (or when you came to Him for the first time). Tell your story.

Realign your heart: I wrote, "As my healing progressed, my response to God's rescue was to know Him more and realign my heart, mind, soul, body, and spirit within His ways." One of the first things I did was to find a new community of believers who actively functioned under the power of the Holy Spirit.

How did your response to God change over time? What actions have you taken to get to know God more? Tell your story.

. . . .

. . . .

. . . .

. . . .

. . . .

Reactivate your faith: I also found I had to realign my life. First, I replaced relationships that took me away from God. I realized that I had used those relationships as an avenue of escape rather than healing. Second, I realigned my priorities in my home, placing God first and putting my husband and my children next. Third, I realized I had a passion for sharing my story with others to bring glory to God.

You probably had to realign some things in your life in order to reactivate your faith. What changes did you make in your life and your priorities? Tell your story.

. . . .

. . . .

. . . .

. . . .

. . . .

Close this time in prayer, lifting each of your priorities to God and asking His help in maintaining balance in the things that are important to your faith.

"I now had hope where there had been none."

Day Three

As I began to live and thrive in my reconnected relationship with God, I also began to adapt new actions to keep my connection to God strong and healthy. As you read my story, reflect on your own actions and habits that you now depend upon to keep your relationship with God where you want it.

Reconnect with God: I discovered that reconnecting to God became the first thing I did when I faced difficult times. I wrote, "I learned to realign my heart to what I knew God thought was best for my life."

How do you protect your relationship with God? What steps do you take when you are facing difficulties? What have you learned in this process? Tell your story.

. . . .

. . . .

. . . .

. . . .

. . . .

. . . .

Realign your heart: I became intentional in how I maintained my alignment with God. I immersed myself in things that were centered on God. I watched Christian shows on television and listened to Christian music. I spent time in meditation and prayer. I worked to learn to hear God's voice and to experience His presence.

How has your relationship with God progressed? What have you started doing that helps you know Him better? Tell your story.

. . . .

. . . .

. . . .

. . . .

. . . .

Reactivate your faith: Even as I progressed in my relationship with God, I struggled to understand the evil world around me. I had difficulty accepting that my relationship with God would not keep me safe from the troubles and difficulties in the world. Despite this, I recognized how I could deal with these outside troubles: "I knew I needed the power of God within me to help fight my battles. I understood I couldn't claim a victory over these hurts and wounds in my own strength."

Have you struggled with accepting the fight against the evil of the world? What have you learned that helps you be victorious in the battle? Tell your story.

. . . .

. . . .

. . . .

. . . .

Close in prayer, asking God to show you opportunities for strengthening your faith. Thank Him that you can be victorious over the difficulties you face because of His strength, His power, and His mercy.

"I learned to realign my heart to what I knew God thought was best for my life."

Day Four

$\mathcal{I}$ stressed that the turning point for me was in being able to activate my faith on the basis of the supernatural power of God. Being able to depend upon His power means that I can now face whatever life throws at me.

In this session, focus on how you've been able to depend upon the power of the Holy Spirit in your life.

Reconnect with God: I listed the things that life has thrown at me since I reconnected to God. Those included: the death of my grandfather and then my grandmother; my father's battle with dementia; my mother's battle against lung disease and rheumatoid arthritis; my husband's business problems; and my best friend's battle with breast cancer. I spent a long season of loss for five years.

You, too, have faced struggles, loss, and disappointment. List the things you've had to deal with below. Tell your story.

· ·

· ·

· ·

· ·

· ·

· ·

Realign your heart: During my season of loss, I learned to depend upon the power of God through the Holy Spirit in my life. I share that this power "was the only source that sustained me and brought any of us through these hard times."

What did you learn as you faced difficult times? How did you depend upon the power of the Holy Spirit in your life? What results of His power have you seen? Tell your story.

· ·

· ·

· ·

· ·

· ·

Reactivate your faith: I emphasized that "there is no other way to walk out this life here on earth than to walk it out with God's power in us."

Do you agree with that statement? Why? Is your story one that depends upon God as you walk through each day of your life? Why? Tell your story.

· ·

· ·

· ·

· ·

· ·

Close in prayer, acknowledging the work and power of the Holy Spirit in your life.

"Being able to depend upon His power means that I can now face whatever life throws at me."

Day Five

Since I reconnected with God, I have spent my life sharing my stories of faith. I wrote, "No one can take our stories from us. Nothing can steal our testimonies of God moving in our lives. No one can dispute my singular testimony. My worst critics and my most evil enemies can't deny what God has done in and through me."

Your stories are important too. Your stories of how God moves through your life are unique. They belong to you alone. As you finish your story today, reflect on how God has blessed you in your life and through your story.

Reconnect with God: I provided three examples of how God has worked in my family. The first we've looked at earlier in this study—the resurrection of my dead marriage. My marriage had become so dead that I lived in one end of the house and my husband lived in the enclosed garage. Through marriage counseling, my husband and I began to see what our marriage could be like—for us and for our children. We chose to believe that God would help us start over together. Fifteen years later, our dead marriage has been resurrected and our marriage is now healed, restored, and healthy.

Think about resurrection stories. How have you seen God resurrect something that was dead into something that is alive and brings Him glory? Tell your story.

Realign your heart: The second example I provided is one of healing. My daughter was given a diagnosis with little hope. I wrote that God provided healing by bringing a man from Rwanda to Mississippi for a conference and into my house for dinner. When he got ready to leave, the man told me that I had honored a prophet from another country and asked how I would like to be rewarded by God for my actions. I told him about my daughter. The man laid hands in prayer on my daughter and, during the process, my daughter was healed instantly.

How have you seen God's healing in others? How did God accomplish it? Tell your story.

. . . .

. . . .

. . . .

. . . .

. . . .

. . . .

Reactivate your faith: The third example I provided is one of protection. I recalled a time in our family when my teenaged kids were under spiritual warfare. One night, my son had been out partying and had a wreck on the way home. He had been drinking and, while driving under the influence, had missed a turn. His vehicle flipped over several times and was completely crushed in. All of the glass in the car was shattered. My son dangled upside-down in the driver's seat, his brow only a centimeter from a metal piece that could have sliced off his head. My son walked away without a scratch, showing God's protection of him physically as well as God's protection of him against spiritual attack.

How have you seen God's protection given to someone to protect them physically? How have you seen God's protection given to protect someone against spiritual warfare? Tell your story.

. . . .

. . . .

. . . .

. . . .

. . . .

. . . .

As you close this time of writing your story, reflect on how your story today is different than it was before you found healing in God. Reflect on how the Holy Spirit is at work in your life. Praise God for His work in your life yesterday, today, and tomorrow.

"Your stories of how God moves through your life are unique. They belong to you alone."

Weekend Reflection

This week, you've spent time writing your own story of redemption, of reconnection with God, of realignment of your heart to His, and of reactivation of your faith. Over the next few days, read your story several times. Edit it and add to it so that it tells your story accurately. Then seek opportunities to share your story—parts of it or the whole story—to bring God glory for what He has done in your life.

Over the weekend, journal about this week's experiences with these prompts:

What have you learned about your relationship with God right now?

....

....

....

....

....

....

What feelings have you experienced during this process?

....

....

....

....

....

What do you want your relationship with God to be like?

....

....

....

....

....

What steps are you prepared to take to grow in your relationship with God?

....

....

....

....

....

WEEKEND Meditation from *Enjoy Today, Own Tomorrow* Declaration Cards

AND THEY HAVE CONQUERED HIM BY THE BLOOD OF THE LAMB AND BY THE WORD OF THEIR TESTIMONY, FOR THEY LOVED NOT THEIR LIVES EVEN UNTO DEATH.

Revelation 12:11 ESV

GROUP DISCUSSION GUIDE

*L*eading the group discussion for the *Enjoy Today Own Tomorrow* journal will take special care. These tips may help you prepare.

➢ Begin your preparation with prayer for those who will participate. These sessions require deep vulnerability and honesty of each participant. Pray for them as they work on their own and then join in discussion on that work.

➢ Not everyone will be open to discussing personal feelings, especially at first. Be patient and don't put participants on the spot.

➢ Some participants may become emotional. That's OK. You will not be able to fix anything but you can provide an atmosphere of support and care.

➢ Always take time to begin and end each session in prayer. Encourage participants to see each time of discussion as a time of prayer, confession, thanksgiving, and praise.

Week 1

Share a little of my story from week 1. Then, discuss:

1. Could you relate with my feelings of "falling apart on the inside and out"? What do you remember about that time?

2. Have you struggled with the concept of knowing God personally and intimately? Why? Does your understanding give you strength or cause you to doubt your relationship with God? Why?

3. I outlined three steps in the process of healing spiritually—reconnecting with God, realigning your heart with His, and reactivating your faith in Him. Do those steps make sense to you? Why? How do you think moving through these steps could transform your life?

Week 2

Summarize for the group that this week was about how anger toward God can affect us. Discuss:

1. One of my questions was, "Why does a God who loves us allow such terrible things to happen?" How would you respond to that question?
2. On one hand, I discussed the impact of long-held anger and resentment against God, and then on the other, I encouraged you to simply confess your feelings to God. Is that even possible? Why?
3. I spent much of my time in this chapter looking at how to pray. Could changing the way you pray impact the way you relate to God? How?

Week 3

Summarize for the group that this week covered the emotional pain we suffer when others hurt us. Read this statement from me: "The Creator of the universe has felt our pain within the beating of His own heart." Discuss:

1. Is it possible to go through life without being hurt by others? Why?
2. What does it mean to you to know that God has personally felt the depth of your pain? Can knowing this help you reconnect with God, despite any anger toward Him or any pain others have caused? Why?
3. I provided suggestions for overcoming personal discouragement and frustration. Most centered around the concept of encouraging self-talk. How can positive self-talk help you reconnect to God?

Week 4

Summarize for the group that I acknowledged that even people within the church can cause us pain. Discuss:

1. Have you been hurt by someone in the church? Is so, without sharing any details, how did that experience make you feel about the church and about God? How did the experience impact your relationship with both?
2. Remember that even Christians are flawed and imperfect. Does anything make it easier to let go of some of the pain you've felt through someone at church? Why?
3. Regardless of how someone else made you feel, how do you maintain your faith foundation in God alone?

Week 5

Summarize for the group that week 5 was about "spiritual alignment," being in the right position with God. Discuss:

1. I used the analogy of a car's tires needing to be realigned as an example of our being spiritually aligned. What happens when a car's tires are out of alignment? What happens when we are out of alignment spiritually?

2. Spiritual realignment has to do with the condition of our heart—aligning our heart with His. How would you describe God's heart and God's character? If you know His heart, how can you align your heart to His?

3. How can realigning your heart to His help you heal spiritually? What things can prevent spiritual healing?

Week 6

Summarize, from week 6, what spiritual alignment actually looks like. Discuss:

1. I described spiritual alignment as pursuing God as our priority through surrendering ourselves and intentionally living our lives for Him. What would that kind of life be like? How difficult would that be to achieve? Why?

2. Because God created us and created the world for us, He cares about everything that happens to us. And, He wants us to come into His presence. How can we do that? How is that even possible?

3. I emphasize the role of prayer, praise, and worship in bringing us into God's holy presence. What would that kind of act of praise and worship look like? What kind of a prayer life would satisfy our desire to be in His presence?

Week 7

Explain from week 7 the practicalities of realigning our lives to reflect God. Discuss:

1. I challenged us to create new priorities and then realign our lives to reflect those priorities. How can this be done? What difficulties do you think you'd face in making possibly dramatic changes in your priorities and your lifestyle?

2. I outlined the hierarchy of how we should arrange our priorities: God > spouse > family > others. Those priorities should be evident in where we put our time and energy. How difficult is it to live according to these priorities and not outside demands on our time?

3. I also challenged us to make our own health a priority. Why do you think so many women struggle with making their own needs a priority? How can this struggle be turned around?

Week 8

Share from week 8 how to discover the gift of the Holy Spirit in our lives. Discuss:

1. I described the Holy Spirit as "the life-giving power that changes our ordinary into extraordinary." Reflecting on the roles the Holy Spirit serves in your life (helper, advocate, intercessor, counselor, Spirit of truth, and the presence of God in our lives), how have you experienced His work in you?
2. I also outlined the fruit of the Holy Spirit: love, joy, peace, forbearance, kindness, goodness, faithfulness, gentleness, and self-control. Which of these are present *only* because of the presence of the Holy Spirit and not something you could do on your own? Why?
3. Finally, I addressed the power of the Holy Spirit in our world today—by resurrecting things that are dead; by interacting with our environment through visions and dreams, miracles, divine appointments, and opening doors; and by giving us eternal hope. Have you seen the Holy Spirit work in any of these ways?

Week 9

Explain from week 9 how we can pay forward on all the blessings we've received from God. Discuss:

1. What does the word *generosity* mean? How have you experienced God's generosity? How do you respond to God's generosity?
2. One definition of *generosity* is based on the idea of being noble-minded. How should that phrase be at the very heart of our generosity?
3. I discussed ways to be generous other than with financial giving. How do you use your time, gifts, and talents to bring glory to God?

Week 10

Share how, in week 10, I transparently told my journey toward healing to encourage you to tell your stories as well. Discuss:

1. Within the chapter, how did prompts lead you to focus on specific parts of your story? How did you feel about that process? Was it difficult to do? Did you recognize God's presence in your life anew? How?

2. Within your story you've probably acknowledged experiences with things like pain, heartache, rejection, and loneliness. How have you seen God at work in healing your life despite all the emotional baggage you may have accumulated?

3. Your story is a personal reflection of how you see God at work in your life—during the good times and the bad times, during the successes and the failures, and during the victories and the defeats. You've been encouraged to tell your story. What stops you from sharing that story with others?

STAY CONNECTED WITH LAINE

Stay Connected with Laine

www.LaineLawsonCraft.com
You will want to visit my website so that you can:

- Sign up for my weekly inspirations that will bring you hope and encouragement.
- Be the first to know about future online conferences.
- Be the first to be invited to weekend *Enjoy Today Own Tomorrow* Seminars, which are intimate and small, to find deeper healing.
- And develop new friendships to help us live the life we love together!
- See the latest tools and applications offered to help further the journey of your personal healing.
- Availability of all *Enjoy Today Own Tomorrow* products.

Stay connected with Laine in real time:

- Laine Lawson Craft
- @LaineLawsonCraft
- @LaineLawsonCrft

Please join the Laine Lawson Craft group page on Facebook today!

OTHER PRODUCTS FROM LAINE LAWSON CRAFT

Angel Greeting Cards:
Blank all-occasion greeting cards.
Package of 10 assorted: $10.00
plus shipping

Promise Cards:
Speak the promises of
God over your life daily.
Set of 25: $20.00
plus shipping

Declaration Cards:
Declare God's Word
over your life daily.
Set of 25: $20.00
plus shipping

Laine's best-selling book,
Enjoy Today Own Tomorrow, brings healing
to your everyday life.

Please visit www.LaineLawsonCraft.com
for more products, online courses, and
online events.

If you enjoyed this book, will you consider sharing the message with others?

Let us know your thoughts at info@ironstreammedia.com. You can also let the author know by visiting or sharing a photo of the cover on our social media pages or leaving a review at a retailer's site. All of it helps us get the message out!

Facebook.com/IronStreamMedia